TO KNOW YOUR SELF

Integral Yoga® Publications

D0171951

Prahaladan (Philip) Mandelkorn has served as a correspondent for *Time* and written speeches for the late Senator Robert F. Kennedy. He began practicing Yoga under the guidance of Swami Satchidananda in 1970, and has been a Yoga instructor in New York, Virginia Beach, Winnipeg, and Washington, D.C. In 1977 he moved to Satchidananda Ashram, Yogaville-East in Pomfret Center, Connecticut, where he has served as writer and editor, and as Co-editor of the Ashram's Teacher Training Program as a teacher of Hatha and Raja Yoga.

TO KNOW YOUR SELF
The Essential Teachings of Swami Satchidananda

EDITED BY PHILIP MANDELKORN
WITH A PREFACE BY SWAMI
SATCHIDANANDA

Integral Yoga® Publications
Yogaville
Buckingham, Virginia

Library of Congress Cataloging in Publication Data

Satchidananda, Swami.
To Know Your Self

1. Conduct of life—Addresses, essays, lectures.
2. Spiritual life—Addresses, essays, lectures.
3. Yoga—Addresses, essays, lectures. I. Mandelkorn,
Philip. II. Title.
BJ1581.2S245   170.202
ISBN 0-932040-34-9
Library of Congress Card Catalog Card Number 77-80901

Originally published by Doubleday & Co., Inc.: 1978
Integral Yoga® Publications edition: 1988
Second printing: 1994   Third printing: 2003

CONTENTS

Preface by Swami Satchidananda   *viii*
Introduction   *ix*

PART I: KNOW THE KNOWER

1. *Your Real Self*   3
2. *The Search for Happiness*   7
3. *What Is Evil?*   11
4. *You Came Alone—Just to Grow*   15
5. *Peace of Mind*   19
6. *Forbidden Fruit*   23
7. *The Disappearing Ego*   29
8. *Wisdom*   35
9. *Who Is the Guru?*   39

PART II: TO CALM THE MIND

10. *Calming the Mind*   45
11. *Consciousness*   49
12. *Stick to One Thing*   55
13. *Mantras*   65
14. *The Farmer Who Loved His Buffalo*   71
15. *Who Am I?*   75
16. *How to Meditate*   81
17. *Tantric Yoga*   89

PART III: THE HUMAN BODY IS A TEMPLE

18. *Hatha Yoga*   95

19. *The Breath of Life*   101

20. *How to Stop Smoking*   107

21. *Food Makes the Mind*   111

22. *How to Eat*   117

23. *Fasting*   125

24. *Heal Yourself*   129

25. *Self-mastery*   133

26. *Walking Sticks*   137

PART IV: THE GREATEST JOY

27. *The Butcher and the Yogi*   145

28. *Business Yoga*   149

29. *The Art of Giving*   153

30. *The Art of Receiving*   159

31. *Living in the Present*   165

32. *The Greatest Joy*   169

33. *Marriage on the Path*   173

34. *Sex*   179

35. *Child-Parent Relationships*   187

36. *Renunciation*   195

PART V: BACK TO THE SOURCE

37. *Life and Death* 205

38. *Prayer* 211

39. *If You Tune, You Get the Music* 217

40. *The Man Who Hated God* 221

41. *The Ant in the Sugar Hill* 227

42. *What We Call Holy* 233

43. *Truth Is One, Paths Are Many* 239

44. *Cosmic Consciousness* 244

EPILOGUE: Old Wine—New Bottle 249

Preface

When you know yourself—your true Self—then you know everything, and you understand everyone. It's not easy to know your Self. It takes work and perseverance. But even that effort can be joyous, and when that realization dawns, you will enjoy your own true nature, which is always peaceful and happy.

May the teachings in this book show you the way to know your true Self and help you on your path. Peace of mind and happiness is our birthright. Why don't we all rise up and enjoy that? Yoga shows everyone how to stand on his own two feet. It is for everyone. It's not another religion, but it may help people find the key to their own religions. It's my humble prayer that you use these simple keys to free yourself from all unhappiness.

The East and the West are coming together. I truly believe a new age is dawning. We can make a heaven right here on earth. But we can save the world only if we first save ourselves, remake and refine ourselves. Let us begin now. The teachings in this book are intended to help each reader refine himself or herself. We are all happiness personified, noble and beautiful souls, each with a unique service. Let us discover who we are essentially and live that in all joy.

I am grateful to the great saints and sages from all the religious traditions from whom we have learned some wisdom. And I sincerely thank the ones who helped publish this book that others may take advantage of this eternal wisdom. Yoga is really the same old wine, only we have changed the bottles for this new age. Here are the ancient teachings in a new wrapper. May they inspire you to live always in peace and joy.

Swami Satchidananda
Pomfret Center, Connecticut
November 10, 1977

Introduction

Yogiraj Sri Swami Satchidananda is a spiritual teacher with a wide following of devoted disciples, students, and friends around the globe. His thousands of followers come from all faiths, creeds, and races and treat him as their spiritual teacher and guide.

"The real teacher is the teachings," says Sri Gurudev, or Swamiji as many of his devoted friends and students affectionately call him. "The Sat-Chid-Ananda exists within every human being." He teaches that Sat-Chid-Ananda or Absolute-Existence-Knowledge-Bliss is the essential nature of everyone. As a world-loved Yoga master Gurudev gently guides his many students to realize this ever-joyous, peaceful nature of their own selves. In 1949, when Gurudev's late master Swami Sivananda initiated his disciple into a life of dedication for service to humanity, that great Himalayan sage named the new monk Swami Satchidananda, the one who is the bliss of Absolute Existence and Knowledge. But Gurudev's path to that point had begun long before, even in his childhood.

Born into an Indian family of pious, wealthy landowners, Gurudev was raised in a devotional setting. His parents often hosted spiritual seekers and wandering *sadhus* or monks, and he became acquainted with them. As a young man, he entered the busy marketplace, operated machine shops, supervised factories, and worked as a successful businessman both in the automobile and motion picture businesses. "I seemed to put my hand into everything," he remembers, "but slowly one thing after another seemed to push me to a life dedicated to humanity and to the pursuit of peace and God within."

When his wife died suddenly, Gurudev no longer resisted the call of spiritual life. He began years of determined spiritual practices.

"I stayed with many great *sadhus*," recalls Gurudev. "The very first was Sri Sadhu Swamigal at the holy Palani Temple in South India where the Swami was more or less our family guru, the one who initiated my mother before I was born. Then I moved into Ramakrishna Mission, from there to Aurobindo Ashram, and from there to Ramana Maharshi's Ashram. Finally I went to Rishikesh where Master Sivananda lived. And probably that culminated my travels—visiting ashrams and staying in each for a while—because there with Master Sivananda I found everything I was looking for. His teaching was plain, open, and his outlook was very modern, suitable to everybody. He preached and practiced an ecumenical way, Integral Yoga. He respected every faith and he always taught unity in diversity. When I arrived there it was almost as though he was waiting for me. He said, 'You have come to the right place. Your troubles are over. Stop wandering. Stick to this place.' Within a couple months he ordained me into monkhood."

Under Master Sivananda's guidance and through perseverance in his spiritual practices, Gurudev realized his own true nature and attained the state of *sahaja samadhi*—absorbed in Superconsciousness at all times, day and night, whether walking, talking, eating, or resting. With his identity well-settled in *samadhi* and his life dedicated to the service of all, Gurudev was soon called to serve ever-wider circles around the world. At first he traveled around India passing on the universal Yoga wisdom, and then he was invited to Sri Lanka (Ceylon) where he served for fourteen years passing on his master's ecumenical message and Yoga teachings. He frequently made visits to the Far East, and was invited to Europe, and then to the United States. His manner and humility made him beloved by people everywhere, and his simple, humorous way of conveying the ancient Yoga wisdom was particularly attractive to newly waking generations of Western seekers.

He arrived in the United States in 1966 for what was supposed to have been a two-day visit, but was urged to stay and continue his teachings here. Less than a year after his arrival in the United States his American students had organized into the Integral Yoga Institute, where they practiced Yoga together. As Gurudev traveled across the land ever more people became drawn to learn from him. To date there are more than thirty Integral Yoga Institute branches across the North American continent including two larger communities of disciples called Satchidananda Ashrams. Although he still travels widely, visiting devotees around the globe, he became a U.S. citizen in 1976.

The simple, yet profoundly subtle teachings of this wise and loving master have already shown many people a way to improve their lives and find themselves. He sometimes uses parables or stories to show the way. "Keep the story," he says, "because behind it lies the truth. It's like a sugar-coated pill." Gurudev is a gifted speaker and a master of consciousness. Wherever he goes, he uplifts and enlightens his listeners. He speaks extemporaneously, sometimes waiting until someone asks a question to begin.

"I never plan my talks," he says. "I just come to the talk like everyone else. I know that Something or Someone is handling me, and I'm just an instrument. There is a Force in me whom you can call the image of God. It's directing my intelligence and my ego. Don't think I have no ego or I'm so humble. I have, but I have given it into His hands. He's taking good care of it and using it. So, I'm never doubtful of anything. Many times I'm asked to answer questions on subjects I've never thought about before. But as soon as I see the question I begin to answer. While I'm answering, way in back of everything I just watch what is happening and say to myself, 'Where are you getting these ideas?' Some people may say, 'Oh, what a wonderful answer,' but I'm thinking, 'My goodness, where is it coming from?' Literally to the very letter I am only a speaker. The person who speaks is different. I am just His speaker. Somebody is playing the tape. That's why I never prepare my talks. I can't even say 'my' talks. He talks, why should I prepare?"

The person speaking to you in this book is Swami Satchidananda himself. As the compiler and editor, I have simply woven together sections from different talks he has given over the years and around the world. I have been recording quotes of Gurudev's talks since 1970. When he spoke at the Meeting of the Ways in San Francisco, I recorded his remarks and later noted his comments to students during informal talks at Integral Yoga branches around the United States. During Yoga retreats in the countryside and initiations of students I noted what he said and also drew from his letters to disciples and personal conversations with me. But almost all the contents of this book are Gurudev's words verbatim, from tapes of him speaking to various groups of people—radio and television interviews in Hawaii or in Europe, ecumenical gatherings in the United States, talks to prisoners and to psychotherapists, messages to his students on holidays, during Yoga classes he conducted himself, and from many, many other occasions.

From the great range of information and advice he offers I have tried to draw out what I believe are Gurudev's essential teachings. I chose subjects he most often speaks about and have also added responses to the questions frequently asked of him during retreats and at informal gatherings. Thus, the book includes such practical advice as how to stop smoking or control bursts of anger alongside discussions on the meaning of God and spiritual awakening.

Between the lines I have tried to retain his style, wit, and personality, for without the man himself, the teachings might sound lifeless. Once during an ecumenical gathering in Florida, a woman Zen teacher sat with eyes closed as Gurudev was speaking. Asked if she were listening or not, she said, "Swami Satchidananda is like a great waterfall. The words are the spray from that waterfall." There is something very refreshing in that spray which I hope to pass along in this book.

Gurudev's teachings are basically simple: In reality each of us is peaceful and happy. This is our true nature. Since we are not usually in touch with this, he offers various methods for clearing away the toxins and other disturbances that made us ill-at-ease so we can again realize our true Self.

I have organized the material into five sections that naturally follow one another. The first part explains what the true Self is and why we are out of touch with that, and shows the way to realize this again. The second section deals with the mind and consciousness, showing how it functions and what disturbs it. Gurudev gives means of calming the mind through various concentration and meditation techniques. The third part focuses on the human body, explaining which diet leads to peace of mind and showing how to use breathing practices and Hatha Yoga postures to cleanse the physical and subtle systems. The fourth part shows how to use these teachings in the world. Here Gurudev reveals the art of living a dedicated life while on the job and mixing with family and friends. In the final section he gives the essence behind all religions, explains what or who God is, and shows how to use devotion and build faith. In this section Gurudev shows how the various religious traditions use different paths to approach the same great truth.

Many people helped bring this book to fruition, including numbers of Karma Yogis who over the years selflessly taped and typed Gurudev's words, anonymously offering their efforts for the sake of others. As I began my part, several people came forward graciously offering to help bring out these teachings. Among them may I mention particularly Swami Vidyananda Ma whose invaluable advice in organization and editing cannot be measured, and Swami Paramananda whose overall encouragement throughout the entire undertaking was great support. Others who appeared at just the right moments as the draft was nearing completion, who willingly typed the manuscript without asking any pay or expecting any thanks for their efforts were Sil Read, Val Bruce, Donna Pollock, and Diana Brinckman. From beginning to end, Anchor Book editor William Strachan guided the book toward publication and added the final polish that helps make the oral teaching easier to read. Finally, I thank Aaron Priest for recognizing the merit in this work and quickly guiding it to the marketplace.

Concerning these teachings, Gurudev says simply, "If it suits you, take it. If it doesn't suit you just throw it away." Over the years some of us have been taking more and still a little more because we find he is leading us home.

I am so grateful to Swami Satchidananda, my beloved spiritual father and guru, for giving me this opportunity to serve with him. The energy of my part I dedicate to him that he may continue many, many years his delightful, enlightening service to all humanity.

Prahaladan (Philip) Mandelkorn
Satchidananda Ashram, Yogaville East
Pomfret Center, Connecticut
November 1, 1977

PART I:

KNOW THE KNOWER

1. *Your Real Self*

The aim of all spiritual practices is to know your real Self, to know the Knower. The Bible says, "Love your neighbor as yourself." But without knowing what your Self is, how can you love your Self in him? Know your Self and then see your own Self in your neighbor's Self. Then you can love him as your Self.

What if I ask you to love all fruits as you love the apple—to see the apple in all other fruits? If you don't know what an apple is, you won't be able to see other fruits as an apple. In the same way, to love everybody or everything as the spirit, you should realize your spiritual truth; you should realize the God in you.

Have you ever seen yourself, even your physical self? Have you ever seen your face? Only in a mirror. Suppose I break the mirror, could you still see your face? No, but would you have lost it then? No. What you see in a mirror is the *image*, not the original, because it is the face that sees. The face is the subject. The subject can never become an object. The subject only sees an image of itself as the object, but never sees itself.

If the mirror should be distorted or crooked, the image you see will be crooked too. Will you run to the doctor crying,

"Doctor, there is something wrong with my face!"

The doctor says, "There is nothing wrong. You are beautiful."

"But I saw a horrible picture."

He brings another mirror that's undistorted and clean, and shows you: "Look at your face."

"My God, I saw a horrible face in my mirror; now it's so beautiful." No, you would not do that. You would realize there is something wrong with your mirror, not your face. If you correct the mirror, you can see your true nature. If you look for your true nature in a distorted mirror you will see a crooked face. What is the mirror in our case? Our minds. To see our true Self we must have clean, clear, calm minds. Some people keep the mirror clean and realize that they are beautiful. Others don't dust it well. Some break it; some bend it.

We are not different from one another in transcendental awareness. This is what we call the spirit or the true Self. When we say "soul," normally we mean the reflection of the Self over the mind-stuff. Soul is the spark of divinity and the image of God, while the Self *is* God. When you make the mind calm and serene, you realize that the soul and God are one and the same, without any distortions, without any color.

Of course, the body should also acquire that serenity which is called the relaxed or pure state. A very healthy and relaxed body with a calm and serene mind will allow the true light or the true nature of the Self within to express itself without any distortion. It's something like a light kept within two shades, the shade of the mind and the shade of the body. If they are clean like a crystal, the light shines forth without distortions. Thus, one should make these two shades, the body and the mind, as clear as possible.

One should primarily take care of the mind because the body is only an instrument of the mind. The body expresses itself according to the desires or the impressions of the mind. Normally, we identify ourselves as a mind and a body. That is why we call ourselves different names and seem to differ from each other. We want to define ourselves. "I am an American." "I am an Australian." "I am black." "I am white." "I am rich." "I am poor." These are our definitions. But in spirit we cannot differ, we're one and the same. The variations and definitions come only when we identify with the body and mind.

By nature we are at ease and in peace. However, due to negligence or efforts aimed at satisfying selfish desires of the senses, we disturb that ease and peace. And when we disturb the ease, we feel "dis-eased." We were fine originally and lost that fine-ness. That's when we became defined. Unfortunately, the moment we define ourselves—or limit the Self—we are no longer fine.

All the scriptures, all the sages, saints, and prophets say to stop defining. This is the process of re-fine-ment. This is the essence of all Yoga and all scriptures. Read the Bible, read the Koran, read the Torah, the Upanishads, the Bhagavad Gita. They all say: Refine yourself. Get out of these definitions. It's the definitions that divide us. If you say, "I am a man" or "I am a woman," you identify with the body. "I am a lawyer" or "I am intelligent"; you indentify with the mind. Each and every definition divides man and man, woman and woman, being and being.

Am I saying that all refined people will have no definitions? Suppose we lose all definitions and all become one—then we couldn't recognize our friends. We would all look the same, talk the same and eat the same. No father, no mother, no daughter, no son. That's not the meaning of real refinement. If that were refinement, we would lose all the fun in life.

Yoga does not forget that variety is the spice of life. Variety is necessary for enjoyment. But if the very same variety is going to disturb and divide us, we don't want it. But even here, can we get rid of it? No, it's impossible. It's a puzzle. We can't get rid of variety, yet variety divides us and creates more problems. What shall we do?

We have to keep the variety and rise above it to see the unity. My Master Swami Sivananda often used this phrase: "Unity in diversity." Remember this point. We need the variety, but we can enjoy the variety only if we always keep in mind the unity behind it.

2. The Search for Happiness

The universe is full of life. You can see the life force constantly. Everything is living; there is no dead matter. What is called inanimate or dead matter is not really dead. This is even well proven by present-day science. Although you can't see its movement with your eyes, if you look through the proper instrument, you see an upsurge of force—atoms moving very fast.

But what is their purpose? Why do they run around? What do they want? If you observe carefully, throughout nature you will find one common goal in everybody and everything—even in the atom. All are searching for happiness. In the case of human beings, you see hundreds of individual, social, communal, national, and international efforts. It could be anything: a carnival, a festival, travel, war—yes even war. The common purpose behind all these efforts is the search for happiness.

When you go before an altar and pray to God, what's the reason? Not for the sake of God, but for the happiness. You want to be happy by making this or that effort. This is the common goal.

Ask anybody, even a burglar who robs a bank, why he does it.

"I want to take some money."

"What for?"

"To buy more things."

"Why?"

"I want to be happy."

Ask the policeman, "Why are you chasing the burglar?"

"To catch the culprit. That's my duty. I want everybody to be happy, not to lose things and be sad."

Ask a man who drinks why. "Oh, I want to be happy." Smokes? "I want to be happy." Whether he is getting happiness or not, he wants it for that purpose. He thinks this will make him happy. The common goal is to put an end to sorrow and keep one's self always happy.

This goal is approached by many in different ways. Some people want to be happy quickly, so they take short cuts and get temporary happiness. But borrowed joy comes and goes. The happiness that we seem to be getting by our daily efforts is fleeting and mixed with a lot of troubles, worries, and unhappiness. Happiness cannot come without unhappiness before and after. We keep trying to find that happiness and we keep missing it. When we finally tire of searching for happiness outside, we sit quietly and wonder, "What is this? Why am I unhappy? Why do I lose the happiness that I have?" If we're sincere and analyze well, we find, ultimately, that the happiness never comes from outside.

You never get happiness by doing something or achieving something—including so-called spiritual practices, prayer, or the search for God. Even God cannot give you happiness. If He gives, He might take away. Anything that *comes*, will go. Even in the name of searching for God we see people becoming unhappy. Here is my answer: Happiness is not to be sought outside. It can never come from outside—or from inside. It can't come; because it simply is. It *is* always. Where? Everywhere. It is just happiness.

You are Happiness personified. You are that Supreme Bliss. You are that Joy. You are the image of happiness. If you want to use the word God, who is God? What are His qualifications? Always being happy. So, as the image of God, how can you be unhappy?

"Well, at least it's some consolation to hear this. You say "I am happy, but I don't seem to be." You don't seem to be because you've forgotten it. That's the reason you are running after happiness.

You have forgotten you have eyes, and you are running to see your eyes. But what you search with is your eyes. You don't seem to know that because you have eyes you are seeing everything, so you say: "I don't see my eyes; I want to see them." You are the seer yourself and you can never see your Self.

The mere ignorance or forgetting makes you unhappy. The basic sin or mistake is to forget your true nature. It's a form of Self-suicide. By forgetting your Self, you kill your Self. So you become unhappy. Naturally, when you are unhappy, things become worse.

With an unhappy mind you look for happiness. Imagine a big basin filled with still water, no waves. Naturally it shines well. The surface is clean and still. When you bend down you see your face very well. In still water you can see a reflection. As you are seeing it, imagine that something falls into the basin. Immediately the surface is disturbed and you see a distorted image of your Self. Forgetting your real image, you take that to be your true nature; you identify yourself with that image and sit and cry. Then you run about saying, "I have to get myself in shape."

You can make the mind straight and undisturbed by taking away the cause of its disturbance. What fell into your mind to disturb it? Certainly nothing from outside can fall in—unless you allow something to happen to your mind.

You allow associations with things or words to fall in and disturb your mind. If somebody uses a word that isn't pleasing, you say, "He's scolding me," and become upset. You allow his word to come and disturb your mind. Then you say, "He is making me unhappy." But really you disturb your own mind.

It's better to say "I *am* happy" than "I want to be happy." The minute you say "I want to be happy," that very want disturbs the mind. And suppose the want is fulfilled? How many people go crazy over a small piece of paper, a stamp printed some one hundred years ago? They pay thousands of dollars to get that piece of paper. They give value to it and struggle to obtain it. If you are caught up in this, you'll say, "I can't be happy" without the stamp. So you pay the price. Then you say, "Ah, I got it." It's simple enough. First you said, "I want it." After all the effort you say, "I got it." Where are you now? The same place you were before you wanted it. Happy.

Understand this well. You were happy before you wanted the stamp. But the moment you wanted it, you became unhappy.

And the moment you got it, you were happy again. So where did the happiness come from? Not from that thing. The thing by itself didn't give you any happiness. You regained the happiness when you took the want back, or when you fulfilled the cavity or depression which was created by the want.

Once the want-stone falls into the mind, you are depressed. A depression is a hollow space. The mind is de-pressed; you have to fulfill it. You create the depression, fulfill it, then come back to the normal level and say, "I'm happy now." So it goes with everything, whether it's an old stamp, a position, a country, money, a name, or fame.

I say, want not, waste not. You may wonder why I have changed the beautiful proverb, "Waste not, want not." Since I always want to be a Yogi, I seem to put things upside down. Want not and waste not your happiness. Sometimes we hear people say, "He is happy because he is above wants." What does that mean? Not that he has everything in the world. If that were so, he would never be happy. It means he has raised himself above wants; he no longer wants anything.

This is easy to say and nice to hear. But such understanding comes only after running around quite a lot, facing failure everywhere and in everything, and finally becoming disgusted. "I'm tired. I don't want anything anymore."

That's why scriptures say, if you want God, give up everything else. Do not want anything, including God, and you'll have God. God is always there.

The goal is to realize your true nature. To realize your peace, your happiness, your godliness, your image of God. Without that you can never be a hundred per cent happy. You will be happy, then unhappy. Nobody can always be completely happy without knowing that *he is happiness*. This is what is God.

3. What Is Evil?

What is evil? Where does it come from? It's an important question to be answered. If God created everything, who created evil? Are there two Gods, one to create all the good things and the other to create all the bad? We've never heard such a story. When He wished to, one God created everything: "Let there be sky. Let there be clouds. Let there be rain. Let there be earth. Let there be plants and animals. Let there be the garden of Eden." And then: "Let there also be a man."

Certainly He must have said: "Let there be Satan also." If not, there's no room for the existence of Satan. Then the question must arise, why would He create a Satan?

For a very good reason. A student who wastes his life going about here and there and not studying his lessons will be unhappy when he comes to the examination hall and must take the exam. To his eye the examiner will be Satan. "You devil! You have given me all these questions. How am I to answer them?" But a bright student will welcome the exam as an opportunity to show how much he studied. So Satan, or temptation, is a kind of test. God has been teaching you, giving you some good advice: "Do this. Do not do that." How is He to know whether you have understood His advice or not? In the classroom He teaches you what to do and what not to do. Then he sends an examiner to test you. Satan is the examiner. "Hey," God says, "go and test him. I gave him a lesson. I just want to know how he will prove himself."

Then Satan, or temptation, comes and tests you. Unfortunately, people sometimes succumb. Then God says, "Oh, I see. You didn't learn your lesson properly. All right, go down. Learn by your experience."

God always punishes you with mercy, never anger. When the doctor cuts away an abscess, it looks like an evil act, but he does it out of kindness. "I can't easily remove this. It needs a very severe operation. Let me cut it out." A kind heart but a hard action. At first the master is all compassion. He encourages his students in a gentle way and with many nice blessings. "Here are more gifts for you. You are a good child. I'll present you with good things. If you pass the exam very well, I'll take you up to the highest grade."

But if the student constantly fails, the teacher will punish him. This, too, is out of mercy. The purpose of punishment is the student's growth. Punishment comes not from anger, but to take away our uncleanness. Evil is not other than God. It is just God approached from the wrong angle. Good and bad are counterparts of each other. Write the word "god." Read it from the right angle, it's God. Read it from the wrong angle, it's dog. It depends from which angle you approach.

Other than the ultimate power there is no evil, there is no good. Things are only approached in different ways. Evil worshippers are punished for their evil tendencies; for their wrong approach. They are punished to correct them and help them know they have been approaching things in the wrong way so they can come around to the right way. Know that nothing in nature, nothing in God's kingdom, punishes you. He has no hatred toward His children. Sometimes a father is a bit hard on his child. But if he isn't, the child is spoiled. God will never make that mistake. He will certainly punish if there is need, but only for our benefit. That's why we say all trouble and turmoil are blessings in disguise. If we only know the purpose behind these experiences and accept them, we will never blame anybody else —nor blame God.

What, then, is evil? A thing in the wrong place is evil—like dirt. A right thing in the wrong place is a kind of dirt, and it gets swept away. God's power is the same—neither good nor bad. It is like electricity. Is electricity divine or evil? Electricity is neutral. It just is. But depending on your approach, you get either its benefit or its punishment. Plug in a lamp, you get light. Plug in a radio, you get music. Plug in your finger—? Those who plug in their fingers call electricity evil. Those who plug in the lamp say it's beautiful. God's powers are also like that. If you approach God with an ugly mind, He punishes you for your devilish approach. But that's all right. Hell makes heaven tasty.

4. You Came Alone—Just to Grow

The world has been created for us to understand, to make use of, and to grow. We can't run away. The whole world is a hot pot. Wherever we go in the cosmos, we're going to be cooked by our experiences. So we should accept this until we're roasted well. Acceptance of the divine will makes us joyous and peaceful. To others it seems, "My God, what suffering he has." But to ourselves, we say, "Okay, that's the way you are roasting me. Go ahead, do it."

The world is really not terrible or imperfect. Actually it's perfect. You are being manufactured here, much better than any Detroit factory manufacturing new cars. You are being refined. If you understand the world in this way, why try to run out of it? Once you become well-roasted by the experiences in the world, you'll be unattached, and say, "Now I'm happy." Then you can advise others, "Don't worry, you'll soon be roasted fully too, and you'll be happy like me."

If you know the purpose of suffering—to burn up your ego—you'll even rejoice in it. Suffering is a way of purification. You heat your mind and body to transform it, burning out the undesirable impurities. Just as gold ore is repeatedly heated and cooled to raise its purity, all individuals are purified by the heat of suffering. So accept suffering if it comes.

This is austerity. But you need not go looking for pain; you should avoid causing pain either to yourself or to others. You should not do violence to your body in the name of spiritual practices. Some do that, piercing the body, walking in fire, and undergoing hardships. But your body is given you for good reasons, and you should not purposefully harm it. If pain comes, think of it as purgation.

You need adversity to know the truth. If you encounter adversity, realize that these are the knocks and bumps that encourage people to be Yogis. To know good, you should know what bad is. This is life. Accept its lessons. Accepting suffering for the happiness of others is dedication. If suffering comes, accept it with joy, thank God and the person who sent it. Salute that person. Touch his feet. But don't become like that person and bring suffering to others.

Learn the lesson from pain. It is a warning about some mistake you made. If there is pain, go to its cause. After all what is pain? All suffering and pain is just losing happiness. You need the suffering to find out why you lost the happiness. Wanting is what causes unhappiness. People want things to be happy. When you don't want things, all the things you don't want, want you. The things you want are like shadows. When you run, they run ahead. You run faster and faster after your own shadow. Certainly you are never going to catch it. If you want things, they'll keep ahead of you—because they're part of you.

But if you are contented, all things will come to you. Walk toward that light and all the shadows follow you. If you get tired of seeking happiness by running after it, renounce all that, turn around, and walk toward the sun. Then slowly look over your shoulder. The shadow you were chasing is following you. The world will be after you if you're not after the world—that's the secret. To your surprise you will see that everything is waiting for you. Name, fame, money, praise, position, people—everything.

If you are content, even your daily needs will come. You don't need to work for that. A person who is totally free from wants will not be like a dummy doing nothing. He will be used in some way or other by the Higher Will to bring benefit to humanity. That Higher Power will take him over. He will still be doing things, and he will be taken care of by the Higher Will through other friends and people. You don't need to worry about you. Your car never says, "Come on, fill me up. I'm low in gas and oil." That worry is yours because you want to use it. So the Cosmic Consciousness, which you call God or the natural force that runs through everything everywhere, also runs through you. It takes care of everything—including you if you don't block it.

You have free will to do what you want. If you do something only for your own sake, the reaction comes back to you. This reaction is called *karma*. If you do things in the proper way, you won't have to face the *karma*. A selfless action won't bring any *karma;* but selfish action always brings *karma*. This is why you were given free will. Below the human level you were given a lot of experiences, a kind of education by the Mother Nature who has been your teacher during all evolution. In your present life you have free will, and you are being tested. You can choose to act selfishly and create more *karma* or live for others' benefit, which is the Higher Will, and does not create *karma*.

In the highest understanding you never had any *karma*, and you don't need to worry about facing your past *karma*. The person who performs *karmic* acts and undergoes the reaction of that *karma* is your mind. That isn't you. You are the pure Self. Once the mind experiences the God within, there's no more *karma*. It's all burned. But until the mind experiences the true Self, the mind is still involved in actions and has to face the reactions because it still has desires.

Desires make you act. When the action is performed, the reaction is always there. That's why Lord Buddha said that desire is the root cause for everything. May I clarify that to say that *selfish* desires are the root cause. It's impossible for the mind to be without any desire. If there's no desire in the mind, there's no mind at all. The mind is like a rock pile. Take all the rocks away and there is no pile. Likewise, the mind is nothing but a bundle of desires—past, present, and future.

The mind of desires is nothing but an illusion, *maya*. A piece of cloth is made of many threads. Pull the threads out one by one, where is the cloth? The chair is made of wood. Take away the pieces of lumber, the chair is gone. Mind is like that, just a bundle of desires. If there are no desires, there is no mind. That's what is called "transcending the mind." The mind becomes so calm no desires are expressed. Desires are still there, but they are not functioning. If you don't feed the mind's selfish desires, they will slowly die. Desires for the benefit of others do not create further desires. But personal desires constantly create others, which do not allow the mind to remain calm. If selfish desires are fulfilled, you swing to the positive side which is called excitement; if unfulfilled, you swing to the negative side, depression. But with selfless desires, it doesn't matter—you don't swing with the results, you always enjoy what you are doing.

Untie yourself. Every personal attachment is a knot that binds you. You don't have to give up anything in this world—only your attachments to them. You may possess things, but don't let them possess you. And don't hoard things—having more than you need. You won't know which to use, where to keep them, how to take care of them—and all this will disturb your mind. If you have too many clothes in the closet and you want to go somewhere in a hurry, you'll waste hours because you don't know what to wear. If you just have one or two items, take one, wear it, and go on. As the Tamil sage Tiruvalluvar has said, "From whatever things you detach, you are not affected." It's the attachment that affects you. If you're detached from things, your peace is maintained. A person who lives a simple life with the bare minimum is free from bother.

To have maximum and endless joy, learn to be non-attached. That doesn't mean ignoring people or having no feelings about them. But avoid selfish attachment. If I address you hoping to get a little fame or a few more disciples, then I'll be either excited or disappointed, depending on what happens. If more people come, I'll get excited. If nobody comes, I'll become disappointed. Either way my peace of mind is disturbed. But if I'm free from that selfish attachment, I can still care for you yet not be disturbed no matter what happens. Suppose somebody gets burned in an accident, will I feel sad? Yes, I will, and I will do anything possible to save the person, or do anything that is helpful—but without losing my peace. If I lose my peace when I see another in pain, then I will need somebody to help me also, and I can't help anyone. You can't bring peace to others unless you first have peace yourself.

5. Peace of Mind

A perfect action should not bring harm to anybody, including yourself. Before doing something consider its effect on your mind. See whether it will bring you anxiety. By disturbing another person's mind, won't you also be disturbed? Your actions should be completely harmless, and at the same time bring at least some benefit to someone. Then they're perfect.

If you are completely unyogic, just move with the people who follow Yoga, who practice religion. Without your knowledge you will soon be into it as well. This is called keeping the company of the people who want to realize the truth, or God. The sage Acharya Shankara has said that our goal is to live in total tranquility. Even while living in the world, live in all peace and joy as a liberated one.

To attain this, he says the first step is keeping the right company. The immediate reward of keeping good company is that you are not in bad company, because you can't be in both places at the same time. Good company keeps you out of an environment where you might be deluded by worldly pleasures. If you are not deluded, your mind will not be disturbed or shaken. You will achieve equanimity and tranquility, which are the qualities of a liberated person.

Four steps, that's all: Good company helps us stay away from bad company. Then our understanding is clear and we're not deluded by anything. That makes our mind constantly steady, calm, and serene. Once we achieve that state we are liberated while living in the world. How simple it is; we only have to do it.

Usually your mind is not calm because there are constantly waves across its surface. Something or other is bothering you. Even if there is no problem in your life, you worry, "How can I be without problems?" There always seems to be one tiny little screw loose that prevents the mind from being nicely aligned, clean, and steady.

The mind becomes disturbed merely by thoughts. All the things that you see or hear through these gates of the body are converted into thought forms and directly affect the mind. Perhaps you see an apple. That won't affect you unless you translate it into a thought, which you had stored earlier, "I know that is an apple. I remember the fellow who brought one to me once and made me happy." From the thought of the apple you jump to somebody who gave you the apple, who perhaps later became your enemy. Or immediately you might think of the first father, Adam, "Had he not eaten the apple, I'd be happy today."

Thoughts disturb the mind. But it is impossible not to think at all. Even to think of not having any thoughts at all is a thought. That's why even a desire to be desireless is a desire. Then how is it possible to be without thought and keep the mind still?

Just find a beautiful thought. Since you must think of something, choose thoughts that will not disturb your mind. Not every thought disturbs. All the great sages who deeply analyzed this problem discovered that any thought based on selfishness or personal desire constantly affects the mind. "I want it and that's why I'm doing this," is a personal thought based on selfish benefit. It will constantly affect your mind.

An impersonal thought will not affect the mind. Selfless thinking or action, which is not for your sake but for the sake of humanity or for God, doesn't affect the mind because you are not expecting a result for yourself. What does it mean to say, "I'm doing this for others' benefit"? The result will go to them, not to you. The fruit of your action should be enjoyed by others. You neither want nor expect the fruit yourself. That's a selfless thought or selfless action. When you don't desire the benefits personally, you are not disturbed if they do not come through. You may think, "Well, I tried it. It didn't happen. What can I do? Probably God didn't want that. I don't lose anything or gain anything."

There is only one cause for all mental problems, worries and anxieties: selfishness. Unhappiness is caused by disappointments? The cause of disappointments? Appointments. If you made no appointments, you'd have no disappointments. But how can you live without appointments? Again, it's only selfish appointments that can cause unhappiness.

Thus, you maintain your tranquility. You neither lose nor gain. The mind is affected by duality: pleasure, pain; profit, loss; praise, censure. If you can keep your mind away from duality, you can still have ideas and perform actions, but they won't affect you. All religions seem to teach this: Do everything for others. This will keep the mind calm and clean.

You may want to build a beautiful church or college. But if you have even a little selfish motive behind your desire, you can be easily disappointed and unhappy. Big charity for little thanks, maybe for name and fame. "Ah, So-and-so built this church." You are looking for a little praise or publicity. If you don't get what you expect, you worry.

The main problem is worry. Ask yourself, "Is this going to cause restlessness to my mind?" If so, even if God comes to you, "Sorry, I don't need you, Sir, because You are going to disturb my peace." Which should you choose, God, or your peace? Peace is worth preserving more than anything else, even at the cost of your life. Actually peace is God. To me, there is no higher God.

Test all your desires and actions. There is a stone on which you rub gold and see how pure it is. From the color you can see the carat. It's called a touchstone. "Will this affect my peace?" No? Okay, let it be. But if the answer is, "My peace will be disturbed," stay away.

It is with this in mind that all spiritual instructions and religious commandments are given—to help you keep your peace. It's also the goal of Yoga. If you should ask my technique, it is this: It doesn't matter what you do, but don't lose your peace. Eat, drink, talk, have friends—do anything, but ask first, "Will it disturb my peace—today, tomorrow, or afterward?" If you don't know, try it. But the minute you feel something is making you lose your peace, then quickly open the door as you explain, "Sir, I thought I could retain my peace being with you, but now I see my peace is disturbed. Please, the door is open; don't hesitate to leave."

If you lose your peace, you won't be able to help anyone else, let alone yourself. A spiritual seeker is like a tender young tree that needs a fence around it to protect it while it is growing. He is easily disturbed and affected. After he has grown, he becomes a great, strong tree, offering fruits and shade for all. He is then accomplished and nothing can disturb him. So know your own strength now and avoid disturbances to your peace of mind. Choose your company wisely. After all, what is the most precious thing? Peace of mind.

6. Forbidden Fruit

There's no selfishness in God or His creation. When He created man, He knew somehow that man was going to be mischievous. So He simply warned him about the forbidden fruit: "Don't eat the fruits of your life. Instead offer them to others."

Hosts of diseases come just by having expectation for the fruits of our actions. That is the apple which was forbidden. We are all in the Garden of Eden. Every action is a tree. Every tree brings forth fruit. Boy or girl, young or old, we are all Adams. The only holy commandment is not to eat the fruit.

If we understand the Bible in this sense, we all become Yogis. We need not even read the Bible. Ask the tree itself:

"Hey, apple tree—how many fruits have you given?"

"Oh, many thousands."

"Did you ever taste your own fruit—even one?"

"Oh, please don't put me in that category. I'm not a human being. That's not my business. I'm here just to produce fruits and give them away, not only to the one who praises me, but even to the one who stones me. Sometimes I even give more to him. Even if nobody comes, I won't eat my own fruit. I'll just drop them and anybody can take them."

Then why are we constantly trying to eat that forbidden fruit? Because there is an Eve inside each of us. The world is the Garden of Eden and everyone is an Adam and everyone has an Eve

—the temptation of the lower mind—inside them. But, don't listen. Listen instead to the higher mind, the God within.

Every religion says the same thing: Lead a life of sacrifice for others. The Ten Commandments teach us not to be selfish. Lord Buddha also gave ten virtues—five for laymen, five more for monks—which, simplified a little, are equivalent to the Ten Commandments. Yoga also has ten commandments, the *Yamas* and *Niyamas,* which are similar. They are a code for keeping your mind clean and free from egoism. Lead a dedicated life. That way you experience the divine in yourself. Universal brotherhood is also the keynote in the Islam religion. If you feel everybody is a brother, you cannot narrow yourself. You become universal and understand how to "love thy neighbor as thy Self."

All of these living codes fall into place automatically when we lead a dedicated life free from selfishness. What is the message of the cross? Sacrifice. The very message of Jesus Christ is sacrifice. He sacrificed his life for the sake of truth. That sacrificial attitude makes the mind pure, which is why Jews have sacrifices in the Bible. Today we understand that we don't have to sacrifice innocent animals, like a poor lamb. Instead, we sacrifice the lamb of ignorance, or the goat that follows blindly. A weakling is called a chicken. A constantly restless person is like a horse. A very stubborn one is like an ass. Sacrifice your animalistic tendencies within you—not living animals which are lovely creatures created by God.

These teachings are for human beings, for the animals and plants are already living sacrificial lives. We treat them as the lower species, but the minute we say something is lower, we prove that we are lower. A flower can never be lower than a human being. It is obeying God's law. The blossom teaches us sacrifice. The tree has sacrificed its flower. The flower sacrifices its fragrance. All the elements sacrifice for our sake. We are indebted to nature—which is called God. God has given us life breath, food, water, sun, and rain. Knowingly or unknowingly, we are using them constantly. We should return all of that by our sacrifices.

Selfless people are the most peaceful. Even if they didn't want to share their peace, others sense it, take it, and use it. So they express their state of peace and remain in it by performing every action just for the sake of the action—not expecting one thing in return, not even appreciation. If something should come their way, they allow that, set it aside and keep it, maybe pass it on later. But they don't *wait* for results.

If you are rooted in this attitude, you are a Yogi and nothing will disturb you. Actions by themselves have no meaning. You cannot divide actions as good and bad or useful and useless. Even a so-called sinful act could be a beautiful, holy act, one that simply must be done. It depends on the proper place, cause, and effect.

There once was a monk who observed all the Yoga precepts. He lived in a quiet forest hermitage. One morning he was just sitting outside on the stone bench in deep meditation, wondering at the beauty of nature, when suddenly he heard someone running. He looked and saw that it was a girl with beautiful, precious gems all over as jewelry.

"What is it child?"

"Swami, Swami, please help me! Someone is chasing me to kill me and rob me of all this." And without even waiting for his permission, she ran into the hermitage and hid in a corner.

A few moments later, a wild and terrible looking man with a dagger in his hand came rushing up. "Hey, Swami, did you see a girl come by here?" Of course a Yogi can't tell a lie or he will be violating his vow of truthfulness; isn't that so? Then what should he do? Truth must triumph. If you were the Yogi sitting there, what would you do? Bluntly tell a lie? Here's what he did.

"A young girl here?" he said. "This is a hermitage. I don't invite young girls here."

"Oh, I'm sorry I disturbed you." The man ran off the other way. So he didn't actually lie. But even if the man had insisted, "Hey, tell me have you or haven't you seen her?" the Yogi can clearly say, "No." There's nothing wrong in it. It's a lie, but it has to be told because by telling that lie he saves three lives. Calculate for yourself. If he had told the exact truth, the man would have walked in, killed the girl, and taken all the things he wanted. He wouldn't simply walk away and leave an eyewitness to tell the police what happened, so he would also dispose of the Swami. And the third life? The killer himself. The police will not forget him. They will catch him, and ultimately he will be killed too.

So it's not actions that are good or bad. By themseves, actions are neutral. Usually it is bad to take a knife and cut somebody's arm. But if you are a doctor performing surgery, it's all right. It depends on the motive and the results. Do everything to keep your peace and joy. Why do you ultimately want that peace, that joy, or that God? To be useful to people, or at least so people can use you. Why does the fruit mature and ripen? So others can eat. Therefore, to achieve such a state, let all that you do be selfless.

A completely renounced person has no want at all. And the minute he stops wanting anything, he has his Self. That's why scriptures say become poor. Either you renounce completely, or you lose everything. Both are the same. If you don't renounce and you are a sincere seeker, probably the world will temporarily take all away from you.

That's another reason why people who are really after God suffer so much and seem to lose everything one by one. Don't think that by wanting God, you will have everything. No, if you are really wanting God, be ready to lose everything. He will take it away because He wants you totally. He doesn't want you to run after other things. You could say God is 100 per cent possessive with His devotees. When you are a little beautiful and you go near Him, He thinks, "Here are truly beautiful devotees. I want them, so let Me have them." If He decides to have you, He will not allow you to have something else.

If you want to see God, give everything. Sacrifice everything, including your individuality. You can achieve this by any means; sitting and reflecting to know these things, or running after all your desires until you become disgusted. It's immaterial. That's why I say everybody is really a seeker, even the person who doesn't bother about so-called spiritual practices and runs after other things. He is seeking happiness. He is also a God-seeker, though he doesn't know it. He runs after it everywhere, then comes back and says, "I just can't get it from outside." Finally he renounces everything. Even in the political field, how many great men have done this? After being frustrated by leading a life of constant anxiety and fear, living inside bullet-proof windows and armored cars, they say, "I don't want to run for President anymore. I renounce the field. Let me go and find some peace."

With your mind you can pray for that peace and that calmness. You can say, "Everything belongs to You; nothing belongs to me. Take away the selfishness from me. Make me happy and peaceful." While you are learning how to live a life of sacrifice, your mind should pray that way. At first you probably can't pray just anywhere, because the mind is not capable of ignoring everything; it's like trying to pray in Times Square. You need a sheltered place. That's why churches, synagogues, mosques, and temples appeared. It's not that God is saying, "Unless you come to church, you can't see Me," or "I'm not in the marketplace." He is everywhere. But you can't focus your mind as easily in other places.

Every religion has a sheltered place for prayer. We only label them differently. Superficially, labels, concepts, languages, and articles of offering vary. The Hindu may bring a coconut and a banana. Another person may bring a bunch of flowers or an apple. Some burn frankincense. Others light a scented stick. Some kind of offering is common in all religions. Dedication and self-sacrifice for others' sake is common in all of them, too. If we ponder these common points, we understand that we are doing the same thing with different labels. It doesn't matter. Choose whatever you like—but do it.

7. The Disappearing Ego

Arise. Awake. Sleep not. We can free ourselves from egoism. All religions are teaching this in different language. Nirvana, salvation, renunciation—all are words for this freedom from egoism.

God made man in His own image. That means God made me in His own image. God also made my neighbor in His own image. God made everything in His own image. Unfortunately, we just read that mechanically. Look around the world. Two groups follow the same prophet and read the same scripture. Each day they open the Bible, read "Love thine neighbor as thine own self," close it, take a machine gun, and send their "love" through bullets.

It is that egoistic nature of man that thinks, "I am different from you. I must have everything for myself," or "My community must triumph," or "My country . . ." It's a type of individual ego based on human selfishness. Keep your mind completely out of it since it's the cause for war, pollution, hatred, political and religious differences—all are based in that human selfishness. Ego can go anywhere. There's national ego, racial ego, and religious ego. Ego is selfishness. Why do people fight with each other in the name of religion? Egoism.

Wherever you see ego, you see division. "My country," "My community," "My race." If by chance someone is born into a particular race, he emphasizes that his race is the supreme one. That is the egoistic shell. Man dreams inside the egoistic shell which is totally dark. He must break the shell to allow the light to come in. That's the main purpose behind all the Yoga practices—even discipleship or the quality of surrendering.

An egoistic man will never surrender. Nothing can reach him except his own pride or more things to swell that pride. He might even appear to be doing many beautiful and useful things. Others may be getting benefits by his actions—but not he. His pride swells and he is in even more darkness.

You have to rub hard to clean the ego. It's not an easy or comfortable job. It might hurt a lot because the ego doesn't want to be cleaned. But if you are really interested in obtaining the light to awaken, you have to submit yourself. Either you clean the ego yourself, or you put yourself in the hands of a good "laundryman." Let him squeeze. Let him rub. If you don't want him to do it, he doesn't lose anything; you are the loser. But when the ego is clean then God can easily enter to bring all the light He wants.

In Zen monasteries, for example, you aren't readily admitted. You may have to sit and sleep in front of the door for a couple of days. That itself breaks the ego. But maybe you are a little self-centered. You say, "What nonsense! There are so many teachers saying, 'Come to my center. Become my disciple.' They are even ready to give me a cup of coffee as I walk in. Why should I sit here waiting three days for them to open the door?"

Then go away. The master doesn't lose anything. It is you who aren't allowing the teacher to give you what he wants. That will happen only when the shell of the ego is totally broken and you can say, "I surrender. I am your disciple. I know nothing."

Once a student went to a Zen master asking for a little wisdom. The master said, "We'll talk about that later, but now have a cup of tea." And he took the pot and began pouring tea into the student's cup. He kept pouring and pouring. It was overflowing. The disciple said, "Sir, you can't pour anymore. It's full."

The master replied, "Oh, I see. I'm sorry. You had better go and empty yourself. Then come back and I can pour the teaching into you." Once the ego is emptied, you are really open because all prior knowledge was based on ego. But until you empty the ego, there will still be blockage. Doesn't the Bible say, "Blessed are the pure in heart, they shall see God." When? Only when there is purity of heart, a heart peaceful and free from egoism—the "I" and the "mine." Purity of heart and equanimity of mind are the very essence of Yoga.

But don't try to get rid of your ego. Without ego, there's no incentive. Even God has a super-ego, otherwise why would He create the universe? Just change your ego. Make it healthy. If you get rid of it, you will be useless. But if you purify it by changing "I" to "we" and "mine" to "our," then you have gone to the root cause and transformed it. Then you can develop a strong, healthy ego.

After all, what is ego? Just the individual feeling, which eventually disappears in the universality of God. Until then, it is your ego that takes you toward God. Without that good ego, how could you do your *sadhana* or spiritual practice. To approach God you need the ego. But as you get very close, you lose it. Master Sivananda used to sing, "When will I see Thee?" and answer, "when *I* ceases to be." To sing the song you need an ego. But when you *see* or face that, you lose your ego; you lose yourself.

What's the difference between the big "I" and the little "i"? Just the dot, a speck you have put there. That little speck is the egoistic "i." Erase it and you are big again. If you want to get rid of that selfish ego, just keep repeating its name slowly, "e-go, e-Go, e-GO!" Note that the clue is in the name itself: "Go." Some riddles have their solution in the riddle itself. People tend to look elsewhere to solve problems when the answer is already here.

Live in the golden present. A little free will has been given you just so you can use it to give it back again. If you submit yourself to that Higher Will, the little ego dies. Then even your body and face will change.

The body is the development of the ego. Mind creates its own body. That's why when the mind changes, the body changes. Every thought creates a change in your face. All body chemistry is affected by your thoughts. If you are angry, the bile flows and the face becomes red. That's why you don't actually have to see somebody act to know what he does. The moment you see a thief you can say, "Ah, look he's a crook." His crooked ideas are expressed through his body. In the same way, beautiful, innocent, egoless thoughts make the face as pure as a little baby's. We are all born with that beautiful face. Let us regain it by refusing to obey the selfish ego.

Sometimes you have to be angry with your ego. Refuse to obey such a boss. Just say, "I can't work for you," because egoistic action will not bring real joy. It may give you joy temporarily, but it always brings even more problems later. If you analyze, egoistic desires will go away. Keep on analyzing: Is it worth satisfying the ego? How long can you do it? It always demands more and more. Where is the end? And meanwhile, you must constantly be alert, watching for tension and anxiety.

If you just ignore the ego and lead a simple, childlike life, you won't have to worry about ego. Why worry what others say of you? You should know who you are. One man might say you are a scoundrel; that is the way he sees you. If he says you are always a wonderful person, will that make it so? If he says you are a rascal, will you be that? Should somebody else tell you who you are? Don't worry what others say.

That's how I'm saved from my ego. Some people say, "You are a great and wonderful Swami." Probably they have nice eyes. It's their opinion. I should know who I am. Other people say, "You are a rogue exploiting the world." That's the way they think. They should have that freedom to think that and sometimes say it. If I don't know me, I might accept what they say. But I know me, so I don't need to worry about what others say. If you know your Self, you're free from this bother. There's no room for an ego that is easily infatuated by others' praise and affected by others' blame.

Would you like to lose some weight? People are usually so worried about reducing their physical weight. Yet, how much lighter and freer they would be if they reduced their egoistic weight. To weigh the ego, just take a long piece of paper and a pencil and list all that you call yours: your name, your fame, your position, your power, your brain—everything. If your list is long, you really carry a heavy load. The less weight you bear, the freer you are.

Suppose I write very little and have only one pen. That's enough for me. But if I'm going to have ten pens and use only one, then I'm practically stealing the use of nine pens which could be in different people's hands. There's plenty in the world if only we care and share. There's nothing missing in the world because it's nature's duty to give us all we really need. What nature will not do is fulfill our greed.

Therefore, detach yourself. That doesn't mean running away from the world or doing no good for the world. On the contrary, by detachment you will become one of the people best able to do something for the world. Imagine, if all the leaders would develop a spirit of service and detachment. The world would be heaven.

The world is for our enjoyment. We want to make use of everything. If we know how to use everything in the proper light and atitude, then everything will bring us health, happiness and joy.

Know that you are going to control your ego. Then you'll enjoy even the difficulties and the failures. After the struggle, you'll no doubt have defeated the demon.

8. Wisdom

As long as you bask in the sun, it doesn't matter whose sun it is.

Understanding is a great quality which one and all should possess. If you understand one another, you will also understand God. Without knowing or understanding your own Self and your neighbor's Self, how are you going to understand God? Literally breaking down the meaning of the word "understanding" comes only when you "stand under."

People don't want to stand under anybody. "Why should I be below? Am I so low?" People want to be on the upper level. But humility comes only through understanding. As long as you think you're somebody, you are not. When you realize you're nothing, then you really are something. When you say that you don't understand, you already begin to understand. It's not an inferiority complex. It's humility. Remember, the one who has a lot of understanding is always humble.

You are probably familiar with the wheat plant. You see the wheat in the field growing straight up. As it slowly grows, the tender grains are still looking up. They never bend down. But at the time when they are rich in nutrition and fully ripe, they are not straight any more. Because there is weight in the head, they bend and bow down. An empty head will proudly stand straight up: "I am so high." But the mature one bends low to the ground. So the understanding one will always be humble, which is the greatest virtue.

Wherever you see humility, there is understanding. Really there is no limit to understanding and learning. In the Hindu faith Sarasvati, who is the goddess of wisdom, is always shown with a book in her hand, still reading. If she herself is still continuously learning, where is the limit? If we are keen to learn, we won't reject anything. You don't even have to read books. If you want to know, "ask and it shall be given." All of nature is a book of knowledge. Draw silent lessons from all around you.

The wealth of hearing is above all wealth. Always listen. You were made to listen. You were given two ears, but only one mouth. That's the proof. Talk less, hear more. If you were meant to hear a word and simply accept it, one ear would be enough, right in front. But the ears were put at the sides of your head, so that when the message comes, it should split into two halves and go in each side. That means you analyze it, understand it, and only then accept it. Don't take just any word that comes as the truth.

Nor is there a door to close the ears. Those funnels that catch all the vibrations are always open. But to talk you must pass two fences; before a word can come out, it has to pass a row of teeth and the lips. Keep words very sacred. Don't let them out easily. If you still want to talk, think twice.

Our understanding is not just through the senses, it's through the mind. Hearing is not enough, you have to listen. Listen with the ears and with the heart too. There's a great difference between listening and hearing. If you listen, you need not take notes. There's a big recorder inside, multitrack, an unending tape. If you listen carefully, you are taping without any distortion. These ideas may appear very simple. But they are the basic bricks with which to build an entire life. Without these bricks, nothing can be achieved in the spiritual area.

Once Avvaayar, a great woman saint of South India, cried to God: "Lord, I don't know what I'm doing. I seem to have grabbed all the things from many books and learned them by heart. I seem to be talking and talking as if there were mouths all over my body. When can I get out of this and find the silence?"

Through silence you can realize the quiet witness within you. That silence is the spirit or awareness. Your awareness is silent.

It never tells you anything. It is just there simply watching you. Whether you do good or bad, right or wrong, it just witnesses. A witness never gets involved in the case and never joins one of the sides. God is like that, and His creation is also like that in a way. Sun is just a witness, wind is a witness, sky is a witness, water is a witness. The witness is there—that's all. And in its presence, you act.

To know that silent witness which is always aware—to know the Knower—you should stop trying to know other things first. Know other things afterward. The rest will come automatically. This may remind you of a beautiful saying in the Bible: Seek ye first the Kingdom of Heaven by which you will have everything afterward. If you don't know the Knower, even if you have the whole earth, the universe is useless to you. All the wealth you possess is just a big zero. By itself it has no value.

Take a check, write a few zeroes on it, and give it to somebody. He won't be able to get even a penny for it. Add two more zeroes. Still nothing. But if you just put a one in the front, and then start adding zeroes, every zero will increase the value tenfold.

Some are very proud of their zeroes. "I'm a doctor." "I'm a professor." "I'm a president." "I'm this." "I'm that." Without that One, the "this" and "that" are zeroes. "I'm a big zero." "I'm a small zero." What good can come of all worldly knowing without inner knowledge? Sometimes, it's even dangerous. First know who you are. Then all the other knowledge will have magnified effect. Don't forget to have that One before all your zeroes.

Know that you are That. Be silent and find such inner knowledge for yourself. Young people say, "To have faith, I should at least have a glimpse of something." Listen to the silence. To realize, go into deep, deep silence. The only limit to wisdom is silence. In that silence realize your true nature. There are no words to describe it. As the Upanishads say, it's not consciousness, it's not unconsciousness. It's not the sum total of all consciousness. You can't talk of it. There's no mark, no symbols. It's not located in one place. That's the essence.

9. *Who Is the Guru?*

If you think you can get the answer and directions from within, fine, do that. Your own mind acts as a guru if it's clean enough. Ultimately, the guru *is* within. But until you are able to get clear answers from within, you can ask somebody who already knows the way. You may have to study books for a while, trying to find the answers. But when you are ready, somehow Providence will bring a teacher to you. When the disciple is ready, the teacher comes.

He or she will be your guru, which in Sanscrit means the one who enlightens you. Two syllables: *gu* is darkness or ignorance; *ru* means the remover. Guru is the remover of darkness. Literally, guru means teacher. All the prophets are our gurus. God Himself appears in such a way, limiting Himself to teach us. It's not the physical body that is the guru, it's the divine aspect that vibrates in the body.

If you ever say, "My guru has a nice face," or a bald head or a long beard, you are talking in terms of the physical body. If a long beard were qualification, all goats could be gurus because they all have beards. It's not the physical features, it's the enlightenment—the divine part in him. A guru is a good transmitter and a good receiver. You receive from him because he has already been vibrating on the divine level. He can feel your vibration and tell you what is beneficial for you. That's why you get guidance. But the outside guru will not actually take you to the goal, he can only show you the way. You have to walk.

If you are hungry, you have to eat. I can't eat for your sake. I can only show you where food is available. A genuine guru will not demand anything except your sincerity. If he knows you are sincere in asking, he will give. Even then, he won't demand you make use of what he gives. He'll just say, "There is the restaurant. If you don't go eat, I won't be unhappy." Sometimes seekers think that if they don't do exactly what their teacher says, he will curse them. No genuine teacher will do that. His purpose is just to show you the way.

It's up to you to make the person your guru. He won't come to you and say, "I want to be your guru." He feels he is still a learner himself. A real guru will never even call himself a guru. Then how can you know a real guru? Such a person won't come forward and say, "I'll teach you." He will simply be living a beautiful life. You can learn from his example. He is Dedication personified, not affected by praise or censure. He is wise. He will not be after things or name or fame or anything. He is one of steady wisdom. There is stability in his life. He is above dualities, not affected by pleasure or pain, profit or loss. He is just there. He won't even force his advice or teachings on you. He won't knock at your door to come read his scriptures to you. You will have to go to him and even prove your interest and sincerity.

A guru is one who is not greedy, who is not after things, who is not doing things for his own benefit, but is totally dedicated to others—always serene, totally balanced.

Sometimes he might seem like a ferocious animal, maybe a little wild or angry. You might lose faith in such a person. You may not know why he is acting that way. He has reasons to bring certain benefits to others. Only a diamond merchant knows what a diamond is. To fully understand a guru, you must be a guru yourself. You can begin to understand him more by opening yourself to him more. The sign of a true God-man is perfect contentment. If you see a perfect master, however, know that perfection is in your eyes. You should proceed cautiously in finding a teacher. I seem to have more confidence in the students who come to me slowly and cautiously. After all, it's a sort of wedding between disciple and guru. When hearts come together, you call it matrimony.

You can't know the guru just by using your head. Listen to your heart. It's a certain feeling, a natural attraction. The eyes meet and they find it hard to separate. Of course, don't totally close your head. A tree is known by its fruits. Just as when seeking a doctor or a dentist, you should ask your friends, "How is he? Does he pull the bad tooth, or the other ones?" If they say he cured them of this or that trouble, then you can be more assured and approach him. But if you hear, "I'm sorry to say nobody has come clean from this place," don't go to him.

Those who are of a joyful spirit are called spiritual people. Those who are after it are called spiritual seekers. The disciples are the seekers, and the guru is the one who guides them to see what he has seen. He is always happy, eternal, stable, spotless, and unchanging. He is the eternal witness of everything. The guru is the one who doesn't pay a single cent, but sees the film always—the Eternal Witness. The whole universe is his film. Because of these qualities he can't be figured out. He's a sleeping fish.

One person cannot be the guru for all. But when you have chosen one, be totally frank with him. Surrender everything. It is for your own benefit. The true guru is not after more disciples. If you meet some teacher who wants more and more students, know that he is just doing business. He should always be thinking first of the benefit for his disciples. He should not in any way bind his disciples. If a teacher says, "You have become my disciple. If you go somewhere else, I'll curse you." If you hear that, kick him out. He's not a guru; he's a businessman. Instead, he should give you total freedom. He may see something wrong in your approach and gently tell you about it. But if the disciple has lost faith in him, he should stand aside in all joy and let the student go.

You should not feel trapped or committed even if you "surrender" to a teacher; you are not a slave. A disciple is a good friend, a child, a patient. The minute you can't enjoy or digest the food that is being offered, you should go somewhere else. If you're not totally convinced, you may stay longer—but not for months and years. You need not eat a tasteless diet for years to know it isn't your dish.

Even if you find someone who is the right teacher for you, you should still know who the real guru is. Remember, it is not the physical body, but the Self, the light within. What you wish to acquire is the way he lives, the serenity he has. Even in the case of Jesus, people should not worship his physical body. It is the resurrection or the divine body you revere and through which you see the greatness and the godly qualities. Then you are worshipping only God.

Ultimately all these forms and names should disappear into a formless and nameless One, who is the Absolute Guru. The form and name are within the mental frame. When you transcend the mind, you can't grasp any form or name. Transcendent experience can never be expounded because to expound you must use the mind. The unlimited One can never be expressed, measured, or defined by a limited one. You cannot describe it, but you may *experience* the Absolute.

PART II:

TO CALM THE MIND

10. Calming the Mind

It's not easy to silence the mind. Calming the mind means not letting it run here and there as it wants. We calm the mind through the physical senses, the body, and the environment. Sometimes we limit the movements of the body, limit our diet, and limit our talk. Little by little we go from the gross to the subtle part of the individual. Remember, the main aim or goal of Yoga is to have good control over the mind. To keep the mind clean and serene is all that is necessary to reflect the inner light or the God within.

As long as the mind is restless and constantly creating waves on its surface, you are not able to get the correct reflection. That's why a tranquil mind is the goal. Learn to control the thoughts so you can create any thought you want. This precise tuning makes the mind your tool. If you can make your mind pure, then the whole world is your friend.

Once you've mastered the art of reaching the mental silence and are established in it, then you can create thoughts. Many people think, "What is the use of me controlling my mind—making it blank without any thoughts? Am I going to be like a stone? Shouldn't I be out serving people or doing something with many responsibilities?" You can fulfill all your responsibilities and serve humanity greatly by achieving this control. If, after finding tranquility, you go out to serve, you are still creating thoughts—but thoughts of serving others. They are selfless thoughts. Even if such thoughts arise in the mind they won't affect its tranquility. That's why dedicated people never have worries, anxiety, or restlessness. They are permanently joyous.

Yoga aims to demagnetize the mind that has forgotten its true nature and now wants to do one thing or another in order to seek happiness. The Yoga practices are just undoing what you have done earlier. But even to undo, you have to *do* something. Of course, you need not practice anything if you haven't done something that now must be undone. So all these practices are just undoing, unwinding, loosening up again, and relaxing. Until you unwind, you'll be swinging like the pendulum from excited mind to depressed mind, back and forth again and again. Once you begin to loosen up again, the swinging becomes less and less. At a certain point you are totally unwound. Then you simply find your neutrality, your center of gravity, and rest.

Even this thirst to find that neutral position—an earnest desire to reach tranquility—causes people to get bumped around or knocked here and there. You know people who say, "Oh I'm just knocking around." While knocking around they get plenty of knocks, until they realize it's obnoxious—or until they finally get knocked out.

These knocks we incur swinging back and forth lead us home to the tranquil state that always reflects our true Self. This purity of mind is what young people call being "high." We're all born high by nature. We shouldn't do anything that will bring us down or destroy the peace of the mind. Left alone, the mind is undisturbed and joyous.

The great sage Baghavan Patanjali, the father of Yoga philosophy, is said to have lived some five thousand years ago. He formulated the Yoga Sutras or aphorisms known as Raja Yoga or the Royal Path, sometimes called Ashtanga Yoga or eight-limbed Yoga. He says control of the thought forms that arise in the mind stuff is Yoga. The aspirant who would calm the mind must carefully follow certain ethical codes of living. The first limb is *Yama;* the second is *Niyama.* These are the do's and do not's. Thou shalt not cause injury. Thou shalt not lie. They are almost the same as the Ten Commandments. Non-violence, truthfulness. Thou shalt not steal, which means not only avoiding robbing others' property, but not even stealing their thoughts. If you want to use somebody's thought, then quote him. Many times we just use others' ideas as our own. Non-hoarding is also in the code. Don't be greedy. Don't hoard things just for yourself or possess too many things beyond the bare necessities. If you hoard more than you need, you are going against Yoga.

Patanjali says that tranquility of mind is the aim of Yoga, without which you cannot gain anything higher. Call it God, Nirvana, or Self-realization. Whatever it be, purity of mind is the most important. That's the requisite. But to maintain the purity of mind, one has to follow these codes. Someone who believes in violence and continues causing injury to others can never be peaceful himself. The one who tells a lie can never be peaceful and pure. The one who hoards too many things can never be peaceful or happy.

By living ethically according to these codes you prepare your mind to receive the grace. Those who open the window receive the light. Those who spread the sail go sailing.

Know that it's not the Self that needs Yoga. It's always tranquil. But the limited mind goes through these practices to expand and see the Self clearly. Then, when the Seer sees his Self and rests in his true nature, he sees the *real face* which is never disturbed. You are the image of God. You are the Infinite by yourself. How will you know when you have again returned to this state? When you're in a peaceful life beyond all dualities.

Remember the goal: Aim at something great. All of you can be Buddhas, Christs, Mohammeds, great sages, and saints.

11. Consciousness

All *this* is infinite consciousness. There is neither the perceiver nor the perceived. This is the great silence. This is the birthless and deathless state.

All that we call unconscious, subconscious, conscious, and superconscious are different states of expression of this infinite consciousness. Just as we have consciousness and unconsciousness in an individual, who is nothing but a microcosm, the macrocosm also has the Cosmic Consciousness and lower levels, which are seen as animals, plants, minerals, and so on.

Take the case of the ocean. It is nothing but water, but the very same water appears as big or small waves, foam and bubbles, ice that floats, and vapor that clouds. These are all nothing but temporary manifestations of the same sea water.

It is this spiritual oneness that is to be realized. This is the goal of our life. Only a human being has reached the level of un derstanding that enables him to realize this great truth. It is he who has the free will to realize or reject this truth. Whenever he rejects it, he faces failure in finding peace and happiness. Such failures ultimately force him to turn toward the truth. Realization of this truth is the birthless and deathless state. There is no birthday or deathday for this consciousness. In this timeless state, there is no past, present, or future. There's no old year or new year. It's Nowhere; but Now Here.

In the human mind there are different levels. One aspect of the mind is always aware of its true nature which is infinite consciousness. In fact, you are split. What you call the true you is different from the little you. There is the big I, and the little i.

The mind itself is divided into different levels. One part of the mind desires something. Another part discriminates. The third part wills. That's the ego, which says, "I want."

The minute you see something—"Ah, that's nice"—and a desire is created. The discriminating part says, "Yes, it's nice but do you need it?" And the third level, the ego, says, "Well, even if I don't need it, I would like to have it." It's all one and the same mind, functioning on different levels. The sum total of all the portions of the mind in Sanskrit terminology is called *chitta* which includes the conscious, the subconscious, and the unconscious.

There are three qualities at play throughout nature and, therefore, at play in the mind also. The Sanskrit terms are *tamas, rajas,* and *sattva. Tamas* is total darkness or ignorance. *Rajas* is the other extreme—restlessness or too much activity. *Sattva* is tranquility, both sides well-balanaced; you are relaxed while at the same time being active. A beautiful blending of both activity and relaxation is what is called tranquility and purity of mind.

These three qualities are not completely different from each other. It is the same mind in different states—something like ice, water, and steam. Ice represents *tamas;* it is condensed, frozen, can't move anywhere. Water is like *rajas;* it will run here and there. And water will not run up, but will always try to run down. Steam—*sattva*—goes up high. Like steam, *sattva* is represented by the color white.

It is the same way with the mind. When you are serene, the mind takes on the *sattvic* quality which is natural. Mind is *sattvic* by nature. But when the mind is disturbed or restless, it is *rajasic*. If you feel dull and sleepy, the mind is *tamasic*. We shouldn't allow the mind to go too much into a *tamasic* or *rajasic* state, but it should retain its *sattvic* quality.

You may sometimes have a beautiful dream or vision that is very satisfying. Is it a trick of the mind? Don't always blame the mind. The mind very often does beautiful things. Sometimes it's a good helper. When the mind is in the pure or *sattvic* level, then it's your best friend. When it comes in the *rajasic* level, it's so-so—problematic. The same mind can be a friend or an enemy.

You should analyze it. Ask, "Will this vision, desire, or experience help me, or will it cause trouble?" Use your own intelligence. If the experience is likely to cause problems, then it's a trick of the mind. Ignore it. But if the mind brings you something useful, take it.

While the mind is sometimes predominantly *sattvic*, *tamasic*, or *rajasic*, one part of the mind is *always sattvic*. That part always talks to the other parts saying, "I'm happy to be this way. Why do you keep swinging back and forth between restlessness and dullness?" The *sattvic* part doesn't swing at all. It's always calm. Even if your life appears sometimes to be swinging, know that you are always united with the peaceful Self which is not affected by the swinging.

Yoga means to become united, to come together. With Yoga you can be united with whatever you want—money, name, fame, other people, property, whatever you desire. It's all possible with Yoga. But being united with everything you like outside you won't be possible until the Yoga or uniting happens within you first. Whatever you want to see outside must happen within you. Please remember this golden law, because what is outside? Nothing but your projection. The whole world is your projection. There's nothing on the screen until you project the film through the mind. According to the coloration of your mind, according to the shape, size, and density or purity of your mind, you see things on the screen of the world. If you've recorded beautiful news, nice scenery, and stories, you will see a nice story outside. If that's what you want to see outside, you must develop it within, and then project it out.

Humans are thinking animals. Man is not just man because of the physical body, but because of his mind. "As the mind, so the man," say the Sanskrit scriptures. That's why your thinking must be corrected first. That's why inner Yoga is very necessary. Therefore, constantly take your mind inward.

You don't have to trouble yourself with others all the time. What you want to find outside is in you. If you want to see God outside, see It in you. That's the image in you. Know your true image. See within; hear within. The entire personality and all the senses must be turned inward to realize everything within, to feel that we are one with everything and everyone.

You see those outside as many because you have split yourself into many. You seem to be split personalities. When you say, "I'm fat," you are a physical person. When you say, "I'm intelligent," you are an intellectual person. When you say, "I love you," you are an emotional person. You identify yourself with many things; instead of splitting yourself, put yourself together. Find that Yoga within you. By the self know the Self.

Don't let your mind control you. Begin to control it by staying away from any thought that will disturb the mind. Selfish thoughts pave the way for anxiety, fear, and disappointments. The greatest power on earth is thought force. But before you make your thoughts powerful, first make the mind clean. If you're sometimes bothered by disturbing thoughts, you don't have to try to drive them away or repress them. Just substitute another, more peaceful or loving thought for the disturbing one. All your actions and thoughts leave an impression in the mind. They leave a trace, like a little seed that slips from the conscious mind to the subconscious to the unconscious. But those seeds will be waiting for opportunities to come to the surface and to germinate. It's up to you to make proper impressions in the mind to root out those other fruits of your past. Nip them while they're still in the bud by substituting positive thoughts and actions for those selfish ones.

And as you think of nice, beautiful ideas, you will change your body too. You can build a divine body with divine ideas. Through your thinking the physical body changes right away. Don't think your body is so different from your mind. Mind is a subtle body, like vapor. Body is hardened vapor. Body is mind made concrete—like hardened vapor. When you freeze the mind, it becomes body.

That's what you did in your mother's womb. You didn't go as a body into your mother. You went as essence and started solidifying yourself. Your mother added something more to that and your body developed. This is another way of showing that mind and body are actually the same, but at different levels of expression.

Although the mind cannot be seen, it is clearly expressed through the body. You have the capacity to change your body just by your thinking. If you are always thinking generous thoughts and doing loving things for people, it will be expressed in your face and body. People will see you and say, "Look, what a wonderful person—an angel walking."

12. *Stick to One Thing*

Concentration is the effort to make the mind one-pointed; it is also the beginning stage of meditation. Don't think you are wasting time if you sit to meditate and notice your attention running here and there. That's how everybody begins. Many people want the mind to be well fixed the minute they sit. If it runs about, they think, "Oh, I'm just wasting my time. I'll get up and go."

That's a big mistake. You can't fix the mind right away. You have to train it. When it runs here and there, bring it back. Say, "Come on," and gently bring it back to whatever you want to focus on. Create interest in this practice. Discourage other ideas; educate your mind. This is concentration. When it becomes fully fixed for a continuous period of time, you are meditating.

People just want to sit and meditate without these preliminaries. But neither the mind nor the senses, nor the body cooperate. The mind may be running about and yet they say, "Ah, now I'm meditating." This is not meditation. It's not that easy. The mind somehow became accustomed to running off here and there. Only after you have practiced concentrating—bringing the mind back again and again until it is well fixed on one point—are you meditating. Then you won't have to do anything else. Your only work is to fix the mind on the right object. Leave the rest to happen by itself.

What is the rest? *Samadhi* or superconsciousness. It will happen naturally. If you want to go to sleep easily, you prepare everything carefully. Maybe you take a nice warm bath, drink a cup of warm milk with a little honey, put soothing music on the hi-fi, prepare the bed with fresh sheets, adjust the air-conditioner. Everything is done; you simply lie down and relax. Now just listen to the music. Don't think of business. Don't think of the movies. Meditate on one thing—the music. Slowly you slip into sleep. This should happen automatically—you're not consciously aware of going to sleep. Once you sleep, you become almost unconscious. You can't say, "Now I'm sleeping," or "Now I'm trying to sleep." In the same way, Yogic sleep is called *samadhi*, which really is only different from sleep in that you sleep with awareness. Normally you sleep without awareness; you are unconscious, In *samadhi* you are superconscious. You know that you are sleeping.

This means you become the Knower even when you sleep. By meditation you put yourself in the place of the Knower. When you sleep normally, you don't put yourself in the place of the Knower; you put yourself in the place of the sleeper. Still the Knower is there. That's why when you wake up, you can say, "Ah, I slept very well." He—the Knower—tells you, "Hey, you slept very well." Then you tell others, "I slept very well." The Knower is constantly keeping an eye on you, he is aware of everything.

This awareness is what you call the image of God, which is the true you. The one that sleeps or becomes restless is your mind. When the mind becomes pure, you will identify with your true image. Then you know you are the Knower. In *samadhi* you become the Knower, the one who is aware. You become aware of your mind sleeping. Conscious sleep is meditation.

Actually, in meditation you are dying. Truly speaking, the goal of all spiritual practices is to die. The little self, which we call the ego, and all its associations, which comprise the limited individual, should die. Master Sivananda used to say, "Die to live." He meant that you, as the little self, should die so that you can live in the Eternal Kingdom as the higher Self. That's what you're trying for in meditation. You are slowly trying to calm the mind. When you focus the mind it becomes ever more precise. It was running around violently, but you are putting it in one place. "Lord, when I approach You," said one great saint, "I come as a big man, all ego, thinking that I am going to reach

You, that I am going to catch You. But as I approach You, I seem to be reducing and decaying myself." The "I" decays as you go nearer and nearer. You reduce and reduce. At last you lose yourself to become one with the higher Self.

This loss is what happens in meditation. In Raja Yoga, the last three limbs are concentration, meditation, and *samadhi*. During concentration you are trying to focus the mind. In meditation, you *have* focused it. In meditation there are three parts: the Knower, the known, and the knowledge; you as the meditator, the object of meditation, and the process of meditation. You are the Knower, you know something, and that is known through the knowing process. If meditation becomes deep, the three become one. You either become that which was the object of meditation, or the object becomes the meditator. Then the process of knowing stops. When the three end up as one, that's called *samadhi*. There's no duality, you've lost yourself, your object, and the process.

For this very reason we meditate on God, or His qualities. To acquire those qualities and become That is the object of your meditation. You can't become That unless you "lose yourself" in That. A union means you want two to become one. There can't still be two. They become one. Which one? Either this or that. You can't put two into one unless they are at the same level, the same kind or quality. Those that are not alike will not come together.

To give a technical example, the receiving set of a radio vibrates at the vibrational frequency of the transmitting station. If it varies even a little this way or that, you won't get the exact music. Proper communication is possible only when the receiving set and the transmitting set vibrate at the same wavelength. That means they should temporarily become one in quality or in their vibration.

This happens in deep meditation. You feel that you are losing yourself. That's why a very famous gentleman said, "I and my Father are one." He meditated so intensely on the Father that he lost himself completely and became the Father. It is a rare and beautiful thing to happen. You are losing yourself in Him. If you don't want to lose your individuality, you can't get Him. Many times people are frightened by this in their meditation. Suddenly they jerk and jump out of it because the individual feeling is still strong. They worry, "How can I lose myself? I don't want that." Don't worry. It's beautiful. This losing one's self should happen in meditation. The ego ceases to be. You die to live. Don't hesitate to die. It takes you to an immortal state.

Be careful what you meditate on. You want it—you got it! As you train and then master the mind, gradually the mind absorbs the qualities of the object of meditation. Think of God and you become divine. As you think, so you become. If you meditate on a monkey, you know what will happen. So be careful. If a person meditates on a world champion, slowly he will develop that inspiration, and one day he will become that. That's why a person who wants to be a famous boxer has pictures of all the leading boxers around him. A person who wants to be a film star, has pictures of other stars all around the house. If you want to be God-like, or even lose yourself in That, you should have the proper pictures and symbols. The symbols you choose for meditation should also have meaning behind them. Choose anything you want as an object of meditation as long as it has some elevating thoughts or ideas behind it—something to make you more open, more universal, and more loving. Something to break you out of your shell.

There are many, many methods and forms of meditation. Continuous focusing of the mind on any one thing, one object, one idea, or one word is meditation. Choose anything you like. The easiest object for you is probably the best. The point can vary to suit the taste, the temperament, the habit, and faith of the individual. You may choose the form of a great sage or saint, Lord Jesus, Lord Buddha, Lord Siva, or Lord Krishna. Or if you don't want a particular human form through which to worship the Lord, you may have a visual image of the rising sun, the moon, or the stars. Yoga scriptures say that you can even choose one of your beautiful dreams as an object of meditation. Have you ever dreamed of something divine, something godly, the sages or the saints, or a vision of God appearing? You can meditate on that by constantly bringing it to mind. You can approach Him in any way or form you like because He is present everywhere.

The now popular term "Transcendental Meditation" in a way

expresses what you want to achieve by your meditation. The ultimate aim in meditation is to rise above—transcend—the body and mind. If your meditation is for spiritual benefit, you have to transcend to realize the spirit. You may realize the spirit through the objects or the ideas of your meditation. If spirit is your goal, you cannot realize it while living at the physical and mental level. You must transcend the flesh and mind. When you transcend, you are no longer a physical or a mental being. In this sense all properly chosen methods of meditation should make you transcend the body and mind.

But you don't have to say this is "Transcendental Meditation." The purpose of *all* meditation is to transcend. It's like having a number of different dishes available to be eaten. Whichever dish we eat will ultimately satisfy our hunger. But if suddenly I take one dish and label it "Hunger-satisfying Dish," as if to say the other dishes are not going to satisfy anyone's hunger, this is a bit too much. Maybe that name will remind some people the purpose of their meditation. But to say, "This is the only way," or "This is the highest" only creates unnecessary complications. It's a kind of fanaticism.

In the spiritual practice, there is no "only" way or "highest" way. We should remember that. Even thinking "mine is the highest" will always create trouble. If you like a particular dish, eat it, but don't say, "This is the only food." The other person may not like your food. Tastes differ. If you really want to use the term "only," then use it in speaking of your goals. There is only one goal. That is to raise yourself to the level of Godhood, Christhood, Ishwarahood, Buddhahood, Brahmanhood—whatever you want to call it.

But whatever method you choose, stick with it. Don't be constantly changing. It's like digging a well. If you keep moving from one site to another, trying out this and that, you will never reach your goal. Meditation is a deep, intensive want. Stick to the one thing that is beneficial to you. Put your entire mind on it and commit yourself totally to realize that. Concentrating on that, in time you will slowly rise above even that one thing also. From many things you get into one thing, and from one thing— to no-thing. Then you realize everything by realizing your Self.

Concentration culminates in meditation. Meditation will slowly slip into *samadhi*.

When the mind is completely still or one-pointed, you realize the divine force or the God within you. It doesn't matter what you choose if you're really one-pointed in your determination to succeed. There is a story of a Siva devotee, Sakya, who was a complete fool, yet became an object of devotion himself. He was not literate, but one day he said, "Everybody goes and worships God with all sorts of offerings—water, milk, flour, this and that. Why do these fellows use all these things? People say that God is above all these things. All right, I'm going to worship Him with a stone. Everyday I'm going to take a stone and throw it at him, and let me see whether God is going to bless me and reveal Himself to me or not."

And he proceeded to do just that. He even vowed, "I won't take food in the morning without first throwing a stone at him. That's my worship." It was common practice not to take food before worship because after eating you can't worship as well, which is one reason people fast on special occasions. Sakya vowed, "I will throw the stone as worship to God. Only then will I eat." And he did this every day.

But one day something happened. He couldn't find a stone. He looked everywhere—he found only huge rocks that he couldn't lift. It was a miraculous test. He ran everywhere but failed to find any stone. Days passed, his stomach would not keep quiet. It was pinching him. Without water or food for so many days, he became very weak. "What a fool I am," said Sakya. "I don't know why I made this vow. Still I should stick to it. But, oh God, I am dying . . ." And as he said that, in desperation he clasped his head between his hands. "What is this?" Everyday his hands had picked up stones, so they knew the feeling well—something hard.

The minute he felt his head between his hands he thought "Ah, here is a stone." He forgot it was his head. He immediately began twisting it. He didn't even care anymore about his own life. His only concern was that he had to have a stone to throw. At the verge of death an unseen hand stopped him, and he heard a voice. "My beautiful devotee. I appreciate your vow, your one-pointedness. You wanted to do something, and you are trying to do that at any cost, even at the cost of your life for My sake, in My name. I reveal Myself to you."

Who can get the revelation of God? The one who transcends the physical and mental levels. That is why people go on difficult pilgrimages and undergo all hardships; they only want God. They don't even mind losing their lives. If you are that adamant or one-pointed, you get God. The story of Sakya proves it doesn't matter what way you reach Him. Do anything you want, but be one-pointed in the name of God.

13. Mantras

Many teachers give a mantra to their students as a means of meditation because it is such an easy and effective method of concentration. A mantra is not just a word. It's a sound vibration, mystic in nature, which more or less aligns the whole system and harmonizes it. The entire universe is nothing but sound vibrations. God's body is a sound body, a body of vibration, a mantra body. Most every scripture says something similar—that God is sound or the Word.

Sages in deep meditation heard these sounds, or mantras, representing particular aspects of the divine vibration, Om. Through generations of spiritual masters they have handed down these mantras as guides to aspirants. Mantras are sounds which may or may not have meaning. By constantly repeating them you are able to produce certain vibrations within you and through all of your physical, emotional, and intellectual self. Prayers and chanting may be soothing to the mind, and for a time bring you into a peaceful state. But mantras have a special value. They are not words coined by people who created languages. They are different vibrations of the same energy functioning in different ways. The one cosmic sound, represented as Om, has different aspects. These different facets of Om are called mantras.

By constant repetition of the mantra you develop that vibration because all the vibrations are within you. Each individual by himself is another microcosm. What you see in the macrocosm you see in the microcosm; you are a universe by yourself. Not only you, but each and every one of your cells is a universe. How many solar systems do you have in you, how many atoms? Countless.

Therefore, when you are given a mantra, and constantly repeat it, you develop that aspect of the vibration that is already in you but hidden. You bring it to the surface, make use of it, and get its benefit. As you repeat it, you get the vibration. It kindles the dormant and subtle vibrations in you. It's not even physically felt. Sound vibrations are more powerful than any physical instrument.

There is much done today just with sound. They are developing dishwashers that employ only sound, not water. The whole washing machine vibrates, completely cleaning the dishes. Wristwatches are also cleaned by sound vibrations. There is now a bath cabinet in which you sit with only your head exposed—like a steam cabinet. You turn a switch and a kind of ultrasonic sound comes in. Within a few minutes you are totally bathed, without using water or soap. Pin-pointed sound vibrations are also used as a knife. Today they are trying to develop a method of surgical operation in which sound is used instead of a knife.

Such scientific principles are not strange to sages who have experienced these subtle sounds in deep meditation. They knew the importance of different vibrations. There is no meaning for those sounds, but there is a purpose. When the man in the car behind you toots his horn, you don't have to ask him what it means. The purpose itself is the meaning. You should think of the purpose when you are repeating the mantra. That's all. The purpose is very important. When you think of universal love, you may know what universal love is, but you should also know the purpose of it. Only then can you apply it and experience it. Then you will know what it brings, since its purpose is its meaning. Mantra means anything that makes the mind steady. Whatever vibration makes the mind one-pointed and creates a sort of receptivity is a mantra. Repeat your mantra feeling its purpose. It should harmonize you, and tune you in to receive similar cosmic vibrations. It more or less aligns your whole system. It's a master key to open all the locks and eliminate all obstacles to enlightenment.

There are many different kinds of mantras. For some to have

effect you must know their meaning, or the aspect of God that is being received. But in Yoga the mantras don't have any particular personal meaning. They are good for anyone and won't disturb anyone's personal faith. They are useful even without knowing their meaning. They have a seed letter in them. Just by repeating it, you get the tuning. With a prayer you have to know its meaning and believe in that before you get the effect. But with certain mantras you get the vibration whether you know the seed letter or not. If you want to get your heart and feelings involved, you must know the meaning of the words. But the purpose of the mantra is to steady the mind—all you have to do is repeat it faithfully.

All mantras are different vibrations of the one common vibration, Om. Your ultimate aim is to realize that Om or cosmic hum. To receive God fully you must become a good receiver. If God vibrates as sound, to receive it, you must produce a similar sound—like the radio receiver and the transmitter. Religion is scientific, it's not just mere belief. That's why science and religion go very well together. To me they are not different. So tune your radio to receive that cosmic vibration. God vibrates in millions of wavelengths just as one transmitting station can transmit on different wavelengths—FM, AM, long wave, short wave, medium wave, and ultramedium wave. You have to approach Him according to your capacity, according to the vibration you already have. So people may use mantras to tune in their own vibrations better.

Sound is more subtle and therefore more powerful than matter. All "things" are grosser than sound vibrations. This is well demonstrated in the Hindu epic of the *Ramayana*. Once Lord Rama was in a situation where he had to try to kill his best devotee, Hanuman, the Monkey-God, who was constantly repeating the name of Rama as his mantra, "Ram, Ram, Ram, Ram . . ." Rama aimed his arrows to kill Hanuman and let them fly. But no arrow could touch the devotee while he was repeating "Ram, Ram, Ram." In the story Rama sent thousands of arrows and nothing could affect Hanuman. They went around him, then bent, and turned back. So which is greater? Rama or Rama's name?

On another occasion in the *Ramayana* epic, Rama's wife, Sita, was taken prisoner to Sri Lanka by the demon Ravana. Hanuman was asked to go in search of her. He thought she might be in Sri Lanka, so he simply went to the shore at the southern tip of India, repreated Ram's name, and jumped. By repeating the mantra he flew in the air and landed in Sri Lanka, twenty-two miles away. He saw everything there including Sita. Then he came back the same way and told Rama, who said: "Okay, we'll build a bridge to go there and rescue her." See, to cross the water Rama had to build a bridge, but Hanuman, just by repeating Ram's name, could simply fly over.

It may be just a story. You don't have to believe it. But even in those days they knew sound vibration is more subtle than physical or material vibration. Rama—the form—is matter. But the name is just sound. Which is more subtle, sound or matter? Which can you see? They are not totally different. When the very essence of unseen sound is frozen, it becomes matter or form. That's how the world has come to be all these forms. The name of God is manifested as form. God as sound manifests Himself as the world.

There's a whole science of mantra repetition. People use mantras for different purposes: some to cure, some to become enlightened, some to become intelligent, some to be more beautiful. Mantras also can bring illness and do evil acts and black magic if people use the same technique, but different mantras. Don't think such stories are nonsense. The same mantra power, like electricity, if misused can cause troubles.

There are mantras both to heal and to cause sickness, to save and to kill. Many restrictions must be satisfied to use such mantras. If you miss one restriction, it backfires on you. People who use mantras for selfish purposes will surely suffer the consequences tenfold. Some mantras are just for personal benefits; others are for the benefit of all. Your mantra should match your vibration or your constitution.

The base or the seed of the mantra is a certain syllable. According to the Sanskrit literature, each of the fifty-one letters has its own specific vibration. Each is a key to ignite a particular aspect of your astral body. If you add all the different petals that are in the different *chakras* (nerve centers along the spinal column), you will find they total fifty-one. Each petal represents a particular vibration which it sparks. Om is the Absolute unmanifested, and the others are seeds for different manifestations. For example, Ram, pronounced "rum," is the letter for fire. It kindles your divine fire. When you chant the word you don't have to know its meaning. It still acts on your system. It's beyond our intellectual grasp, but still it works. Such is the power of the seed mantras.

If you go to Tibet you may hear people constantly repeating the mantra: "Om Mane Padme Hum, Om Mane Padme Hum." Almost all Buddhists there use only that mantra. In the Hindu system, however, it's not the same food for everybody. Mantras are selected for each individual. Some common mantras are like a general tonic that you can take without a prescription from the doctor. But *special* medicine must be prescribed.

Some people ask, "Why do I need a guru? Can't I repeat a mantra myself? Can't I select my own?" If you can diagnose your disease and select the right medicine, go ahead. Unfortunately, even then you cannot buy such medicine without a prescription signed by the doctor. That's why the guru acts as the doctor. He diagnoses you. You don't always have to hold a person's hand to know his pulse. He feels your vibration and says this "medicine" is the best tonic for you. If you want a personal mantra, a guru may initiate you.

You have to pay a high price for a personal mantra—though not in the way of a monetary offering—which some people do charge, I'm sad to say. The real price you must pay is that of your own practice. You can only spread the vibration through your system by frequently and regularly repeating the mantra.

To turn milk into yogurt, you need a little culture. The cultured man will put a little culture in you. He has first cultivated the culture in himself. But he will not put the seed into just any soil. He has to prepare the soil well to receive the seed. That's why a ceremony, an initiation, is important. The guru prepares your body, your mind—everything. When the field is ready, he sows the seed, puts in the culture, and explains how to develop it. Through your practice you must cultivate the culture within you until all of you has become cultured.

The mantra is also like a little dynamo. The charging station may charge your battery, but you must keep it charged or it will soon run down. By repeating your mantra you keep it well charged and spread it through your system until its vibration pervades your body and mind. Your entire personality vibrates on that beautiful wavelength and automatically attracts similar vibrations. You become in tune with those who have similar waves, and ultimately in tune with the cosmic wave.

This is the scientific explanation of Mantra Yoga. Until such time as you receive an initiation from a qualified person, there's nothing wrong with repeating a mantra. There are some general mantras that all can use. Some simple and very efficacious ones are *Hari Om* or just *Om* or *Om Shanti*. Don't try long mantras. The smaller the stuff, the greater the power.

Hari Om is a beautiful mantra which can evoke the sound vibration within you. *Ha* is pronounced as in "hot"; *ri* as in "repeat." The *ha* comes from the solar plexus area. When you say *ri*, the sound comes up. *O* vibrates your entire skull. The minute you say *mmmm*, the vibration goes up further. As the sound goes higher and higher you rise above body and mind.

Understand that this is not connected with any particular religion. You are just working with some sounds. Of course, not everybody will be satisfied with mantras as a focus for concentration. Everyone has a different capacity and different taste. There's no one thing especially suited to everybody except the process of concentration itself.

14. The Farmer Who Loved His Buffalo

The sage Patanjali said there are hundreds of varieties of meditation. You don't even have to repeat a mantra or look at anything—if you like, you can just concentrate on the breath itself. Meditating on the incoming and outgoing breath has become an important form of meditation in Buddhist philosophy, and is widely practiced today by Burmese Buddhists.

If you learn meditation in Burma, you are first asked to concentrate on the up and down movements of the stomach. You are even allowed to put your hand there. If you can't concentrate on the breath, you should concentrate on the stomach as it moves during breathing. Later you can listen to the sound of the breath. At that point you will hear the mantra "so-hum," or "hamsa." It is the sound of the breath. After some time the flow of breath reduces. At one point, you experience complete stillness—no breath at all. Don't think you're dying. Good concentration brings this retention naturally. You don't repeat anything. You don't inhale. It just stops.

Have you noticed that when your mind is agitated you breathe heavily? With *pranayama* or certain Yogic breathing practices, the breath is controlled, and this automatically calms the mind. It works the other way too. By quieting the mind through concentration, you can control your breathing. If you suddenly observe your breath when you are deeply engrossed in reading or concentrating on some problem, you may be surprised to see that you are almost not breathing at all. When the mind focuses on something, breathing slows.

Many forms of meditation are available. It doesn't matter which one you choose because they lead to the same goal. If you hold one link of a chain and pull, the entire chain comes to you. You may hold the chain anywhere and start pulling. One teacher might tell you, "Hold this link and pull." Another might say, "No, no, hold over here, pull *this* link. Only then will the chain come." But a wise teacher will say, "All the links are part of the same chain; it doesn't matter where you pull." If you have a link, go ahead and pull. I'm just quoting the authority, Patanjali. Even then he knew someone might come along who wouldn't like the ways he offered and say: "I'm not truly interested in any of those methods. Maybe I'm not built for meditation. Isn't there anything else?"

Expecting such a question, Patanjali said, Okay, whatever is tasteful to you, meditate on that. One time a student who was a farmer once came to Ramakrishna Paramahamsa and said, "You say meditate on God and use this mantra. I'm not interested in God and mantras. I don't know who He is or what a mantra is. Without knowing anything about them why should I use them? How can I meditate on something like that? I can't go on a guess. Can't I meditate on something that I know about?"

Ramakrishna asked, "What is very dear to you?" He knew that you can't meditate on something you don't like. You must love the object of your meditation. If you are always thinking about the one you love most, then your meditation will be easy.

"Oh, I'm just a farmer. I have a nice buffalo at home. I love that buffalo. I love many things, but if you ask me to to compare them, the buffalo is the most beloved of them all."

"That's fine. You have something which for you is the most beloved. Meditate on your buffalo."

"Swami, are you really sure?"

"Yes, meditate on your buffalo."

"That's easy for me."

"Go and do it then."

He went home, took his buffalo into a nice room, tied it there, and simply sat watching the buffalo. The buffalo was watching him too. Soon he could visualize his beautiful beloved buffalo. It would appear in his visions because as you know, when you love somebody, there's no difficulty in creating that image. If by chance you see somebody in the supermarket, who you love, you simply find it hard to forget that face afterward. It comes in your dreams, doesn't it?

So meditation was easy for the farmer. He just sat there and got the vision while the buffalo was simply wagging his tail. He got so involved that he forgot sleep and food. He was totally drawn in. His concentration was so deep that soon he felt he himself was the buffalo.

That is the fruit of your meditation. When you meditate on something you should become that object. Though your intellect can't make you that object, even without your knowing it you come to feel you are that already. You forget your own entity or individuality and say, "I am that."

The farmer felt that he had become the buffalo. He was enjoying the buffalo meditation, but his wife was scared. She ran to Ramakrishna and said, "My husband doesn't even want to come out of the room. He's just sitting there. He seems to have forgotten everything else. He doesn't eat; he doesn't sleep. Two or three days have passed. I don't know what to do with him."

Ramakrishna immediately went to see the farmer. His student was sitting in deep meditation. "Hello, I'm Ramakrishna, would you like to come out?"

"Swami, I would come, but unfortunately my horns are so wide, I can't leave this room." In his mind he had these great buffalo horns that would not pass through the door.

"Is that so? Okay, chop off those horns."

"Do you really want me to do that?"

"Yes. You have to come out. Chop them off."

"Okay." And in his imagination he chopped off the horns. Then he tried to move. His head emerged from the room but his body wouldn't follow. "I have grown so big, my body won't go through the door."

"Well you have to come out. You can't always sit in the room."

"I don't know what to do, Swami."

"Come on, take the sword. Chop off the head. The head is more important than the body. Chop it off and come out."

In his mind the farmer did so. And when the head was chopped off, the animal died. The farmer returned from a beautiful meditation.

Meditate on what you like. Choose anything. But if you meditate on the buffalo you will have the problems of chopping off the horns and the head. It's nice to meditate on the light right away. If you do, you won't need to undergo the process the farmer went through.

Of course some teachers say, "This is best to meditate on." Why? To create more interest for you. It's not that they're all fanatics. Unless you are told "what I am giving you is the very best ever done," you may not cherish it enough. When you cherish it, you will be motivated deeply. Unfortunately, sometimes seekers get a method from their teachers, but don't work on it. They just talk about it. "Hey, I got this. It's the very best form of meditation. What are you meditating on?"

The other says, "I'm just meditating on this."

"Nonsense. That's not good. Mine is the best." Such students don't meditate. They brag about their method, but they never do it. It's as if you have the fruit. You don't eat it, you tell people, "I have the fruit. This is the best fruit in the world."

"Oh, can I have it?"

"No, no, no, no." Neither do you eat, nor do you allow him to eat. Yet you take it around and talk about it. That's why some teachers ask you not to talk about what you are doing, but to keep it a secret and work with that. Unfortunately, some teachers don't know the tendencies of their students and fail to warn them not to advertise. "I have given this to you. Now his is yours. Keep it. Use it. But don't start acting as my public relations man." Many students think they are public relations people or that they immediately are teachers. That's a dangerous kind of fanaticism.

It doesn't matter what you choose. Take it. Use it. Ultimately you are going to get it. If you simply talk about it and wonder about it—or advertise it—self-realization will take quite a long time. But if you are serious, sincere, and persistently practice whatever method you have chosen, self-realization comes quickly.

15. Who Am I?

Deep in the middle of the ocean of the mind there is no pollution. It is absolutely pure. That part is always contented. It never likes or dislikes. It accepts everything; it is not proud. And this is the real nature of your true Self. Only knowledge of this true nature will free you from the turmoil of this world. It will free you from the petty-mindedness which divides humanity into thousands of names: "I am this; he is that. He is different from me." People kill each other because they group and divide themselves. They fail to see and know that they are above these differences.

By knowing your true identity you can also know others. We come together in that knowledge. This goal is expounded by all great philosophies and by all teachings in Yoga. Contemplating and analyzing these points is another form of meditation, called Jnana Yoga or the Yoga of Wisdom that comes of self-analysis. It is well-suited to the temperament of analytical people. In this practice you simply sit and analyze everything that has happened and everything that is happening. That way you detach yourself and rise above your limitations. "Who am I? How do I know all these things? I know that I'm disturbed. Yet my knowing doesn't seem to get disturbed. If I am disturbed, who is it that knows something is disturbed in me?"

If a madman knows that he is mad, he is not mad. If a dreaming man knows that he is dreaming, he's not dreaming. If an insane man recognizes his problems and says, "You know, I'm insane," he is immediately discharged from the asylum. The minute you know you are diseased, you are already on the path of recovery. Ignorance of a disease is its main cause.

Whenever something happens to you, ask why. But don't be too serious in your practice. When a friend comes to say hello, don't continue your analysis. You may temporarily set aside the questioning—Who is he? Who am I?—for the sake of maintaining good relationships and dealing with people and things.

The analytical person always questions everything. That person takes a fruit, and immediately asks, "Who planted it? Where did it come from? The tropics? Arctic? Atlantic? What is the cost? How long will it last?" He won't even eat the fruit before answering all these questions.

His mother says, "Child, I'm your mama."

"How am I to know that? You mean to say I should believe you? Give me proof."

Or his mother might say, "Mr. So-and-so is your father."

"Are you sure? I can't take your word." He wants to put everything into a test tube for direct analysis. He questions everything, both external and internal. "Who am I? Why am I? Since when have I been called Jacob? Only since my parents gave me that name. Who was I before that? I was just a baby and given the name, 'child.' Sometime later, they gave me the name Jacob. Who am I, then, a child or Jacob?" He wants to analyze everything. "I write my name with an adjective next to it—'President.' Since when am I President, and how long am I going to be President? Since when am I a lawyer? What was I before? Suppose some great shock comes to my brain. If I forget all these legal ideas, will I still be a lawyer or President? Or will I be in an asylum? So what are these names? How did I get these names?"

By such questioning he comes to understand that he is completely different from the body and from the mind, from its feelings and its actions. If he feels angry, he asks, "Where is the anger?" At least it is not in the body though it may express itself in the body later. The feeling is in the mind where it is expressed as mental agitation. How do you *know* that you are angry? If the person knows, then he is not angry. The one who knows isn't the angry one. The mind is angry. The Knower isn't angry.

If you can say, "I know I am disturbed," there's no disturbance in your knowing that you are disturbed. The direct analysis approach of Jnana Yoga is very subtle. If your very knowing is disturbed you can never know that you are disturbed. You knew that you were happy. Now you know that you are unhappy. You know everything that is happening in you. This *knowing* is called awareness or consciousness. The true person, the true you is constantly the same because there is no change in that knowing. You knew you were a child. Now you know that you are an adult, and you know you are going to be an old man or an old woman. The *knowledge* of childhood, adulthood, and old age is the same. You are not really isolated or separated. You are only temporarily identifying yourself as the body. If I ask you what you are doing, you can say, "I'm sitting down," but *you* are not sitting. Your body is seated. When you say "I fell down," who is this "I"? Certainly not the real I. The differences of the body make your mind feel different, and you identify yourself as the body.

This self-analysis can solve all your problems. You are not your body. You are not your mind because you are the one who is observing them. Whatever it is that is bothering you—anything at all—sit back and ask yourself, "What did I do? What mistakes have I made? Where was I selfish?" When you analyze in this way you will see that your happiness does not come from outside you. Your mind and body continue to go through some changes, but knowing doesn't change. The peaceful nature is never affected. Only when you forget and identify yourself with the body or the mind do the clouds come and block your view of the sun—the true Self. The sun is always shining whether the clouds are there or not. The mind may pass through some of these cloudy periods, but as the Knower, you can enjoy the show. Enjoy the mind and its play. After all, it's the mind. There's nothing wrong with it going through changes. Sometimes it's happy, sometimes unhappy. You know that. No need to worry about that. Just let it go and enjoy the show. It's always a beautiful play to be seen.

Everybody is an actor. The world is the biggest theater. If we learn to act our parts well, we really enjoy the show. Now I'm acting as a guru. I'm playing my part. But who makes the guru? The disciples, the students. In dramatic truth, we're all in a great play. But there's only one super-director, the puppet master who pulls the strings to make us dance. The Cosmic Consciousness just separates itself into many plays and players and then dissolves back again. Play your part without forgetting your identity. If you know the true identity of others too, you'll have fun. Don't think that spiritual life is so hard. It should all be fun.

So watch your mind. Watch your breath. Become an observer, which is the key to this form of meditation. Don't worry about particular techniques. Just sit back observing the breath, mind, and thoughts. Just see what's happening within you. Become a witness, which is a wonderful form of meditation. Be still and watch what is happening in your mind and in your body. Maybe you have been repeating a mantra or focusing on one object for a time. You may then relax and sit calmly and watch the mind; observe the peaceful vibrations that come. Listen to the silence completely. Observe your own brain. See how peaceful you are. The mind seems to be totally at rest. You might think the mind is almost asleep, yet you are still conscious of the whole thing. The body is resting. The breath has very much slowed. The mind is almost sleeping but you are aware of everything.

Who is aware of them? What is this awareness? Who knows all these things? That is *You.* You are totally different from your body, from your mind. You are the witness—what you call the Self, the Pure Self—the witness of the body and mind. If you could maintain this witnessing constantly, still knowing you are that witness all the time, you would have reached self-awareness or self-realization. Keep up this awareness, even in your day-to-day activities. When you are eating, you can still witness: "Here I am taking the food, chewing the food, tasting the food." You will constantly enjoy supreme peace. Through this you become the master of your own body and mind. You'll walk like an undisturbed sage.

Find out who you are. Once you know who you are, you will be the best instrument to bring peace and harmony to all. Ultimately you will find you are not somebody who is going up and down, but that you are a permanent entity, an image of God.

I don't know whether I am making sense to you. All I know is that I feel so easy and peaceful. I never become depressed or excited. No worries. That's my great wealth. What else do you need? All things are just part of nature, which can do anything and everything. The mind and body are also part of nature. Nature changes, so they too must constantly change. Allow them to play their part. Be a witness—the Eternal Witness.

That doesn't mean you'll be useless to people. You'll see that you will be doing things perfectly because you have become a beautiful instrument and everything will want to come to you, to be used by you and to make use of you. You never take sides. You become the total, neutral person. Neutrality is the center of God, the center of nature. From there, according to the need, you can go this way or that way without losing your center.

16. How to Meditate

Whenever you feel in a peaceful state of mind, meditate. Just close your eyes and relax, even if it's only for a minute. If you wish to deepen your meditation, then schedule some time for this practice daily. Meditation needs the co-operation of both the body and the mind. Prepare the body with the *asanas* or Yoga postures and *pranayama*, breathing exercises. As for the mind, learn to keep it always fully occupied on one thing, but don't let that thing or concept bind you.

Stick to one object of concentration, don't change continually. It's best to be regular in practicing meditation—try to have two sittings daily. The scriptures recommend the times when day meets night or night meets day for meditation—dawn and dusk. It's neither day nor night and thus very conducive. If this is not possible, sit as soon as you wake in the morning and at night before retiring.

If you get up after the world is already awake, it's probably best to quiet yourself by first doing the Yoga postures and some breathing practices. Then go on to your meditation. In this way you go from the physical to the mental, and from the mental to the spiritual. It's easy to go from the gross to the subtle. If you wake very early in the morning, before dawn, it is already very *sattvic* or peaceful. Don't disturb this with any physical practices; begin your meditation immediately.

Even in the midst of Hatha Yoga *asanas* you may sometimes feel so very peaceful that you can simply stop doing the postures and enjoy that pleasant meditation. When you're actually trying to meditate, be very gentle. Training the mind to stay on one point is something like training a horse. If the horse doesn't want to go into a particular lane, you can't force it. It will revolt. A tricky trainer will say, "All right, where do you want to go? This way? Sure, turn." You let the horse go a few yards that way, then slowly you take him around. The horse is pleased: "Ah, I had my way." Very soon the trainer will say, "I have my way now."

Your mind is something like that. Just bring it around. Otherwise the mind will build a block of tension, and from the moment you even think of meditating, it might create psychosomatic illnesses. You might feel a little headache or a stomach-ache. The mind has that power. You shouldn't force the mind up to any level, but at the same time don't give it too much rope either. It's kind of a middle path. Be firm and at the same time gentle.

You should choose a nice clean place for your regular sitting, on something that is a non-conductor of electricity. You may have heard of Yogis in India who sit on a wooden platform or on a certain grass that does not conduct any electricity. This more or less acts as insulation from the gravitational force of the earth. Have you seen pictures of Yogis sitting on animal skins? They didn't kill those animals for the skins, they just used what was available. For forest Yogis it was natural to use a dry, tanned skin, like the non-conducting gloves you might wear when handling electricity.

Often they chose tiger and deer skins. It is believed that if you sit on a deerskin and meditate you will acquire all the aesthetic beauties, the charms of life, and liberation too. If you sit on a tiger skin, you get all the *siddhis* or attainments and supernatural powers. Tiger skin brings power because the skin has its own vibration also. If the animal has died naturally, the skin will still have the quality or the nature of the animal. If you use a deer skin, you get the soft or gentle nature of the deer. Even if you wear a dress with the pattern of a tiger, you walk like a tiger. Immediately you feel you are a tiger yourself. It's thought association.

Unfortunately, those old practices have descended to a low

level today. Many people want to meditate on an animal skin, and this has been propagated by the people who are selling the skins. Certainly you can't get helpful qualities from animals that have been slaughtered. I personally don't like to use a skin for meditation. I don't know whether the animal has been killed or died naturally. If I buy it, I will be encouraging people to kill more. I would suggest a clean white sheet, folded over a blanket or carpet. Use this only for your meditation practice and it will build up wonderful vibrations.

Preparing the body for meditation is also important. In meditation you are trying to keep the mind steady and one-pointed without shaking too much. To do this you begin by making the body steady. This is possible only if you make a firm decision. Just tell the body and the limbs, "I'm not going to move any part of the body until I finish the meditation." The decision you make will be heard by every cell in your body. If the decision is very strong, the body will obey you without complaining. Imagine your mind and body as little children. If you want them to obey, you must be a little firm.

It's best to sit in a cross-legged posture. Sit straight. Keep the spine erect but not stiff. Spread the chest well. Beginners may find this position easier if they sit on the edge of a firm cushion. If this isn't possible, it's all right to use a chair, but keep the spine free by not leaning back on it.

It's normal to feel some pain in a cross-legged position when you begin. Slowly, slowly you will get over it. The minute you feel the pain, change the position of your legs. Sit some other way that's more comfortable for you, and continue your meditation. This doesn't mean you should avoid sitting or meditating. Each day sit to that point where you feel the pain, then shift to another position.

You can even get up while meditating and walk around a little. Then sit a while longer. Once you find the real center of gravity—your equilibrium—you'll have victory over the position and be seated in a steady and comfortable pose. Build your meditation little by little.

How long should you sit? If it's a deep meditation, five or ten minutes is enough. If it's not deep, stay longer. Begin by sitting for fifteen minutes. In fifteen days you can easily sit twenty minutes each time. Twenty will become twenty-five then thirty. Nothing is built in one day. Everyone who has learned to meditate has gone through these same steps.

If in meditation you are sometimes bothered by intruding thoughts or desires, sometimes the best thing to do is to meditate on the very desire itself. Of course, you can first try to ignore it. But that might not work. A simple example: You are in a room and you are doing something intensely. All of a sudden somebody walks in without an appointment. You look at him out of the corner of your eye and realize this is not the time to see him, or he is not desirable now. You could say, "Don't come in without an appointment—get out!" Then he won't be going away happily. You are making an enemy. He might bang the door as he leaves and go outside and shout. If you reject a strong desire, it won't go away, but will wait for another opportunity to pounce on you when you are a bit weak. Don't force it out.

If you know someone is there, don't even look at him. Seem to be very busy—deeply, deeply interested in something. Even when he says, "Sir?" you do not seem to hear him. You are very busy. Get even more involved in your concentration. He will wait some time, then say, "I see. He seems to be very busy. I will come another time." And he'll walk out.

On the other hand, if he's persistently waiting for your attention—even beyond your patience—then turn to him, "Yes, sir, what can I do for you?" Analyze the desire. If you can't do what he wants right away, tell him, "Yes I will certainly do that, but not just now. Come again another time." By analyzing it, you can either dispose of the desire or settle the matter quickly. Suppose you are meditating and you feel the desire to eat or go to the movies, which you can't ignore. Then face it: "All right, you want to take me to the movies. How many films have we seen lately? With what benefit? What's new today? Will this be greater benefit than that from meditation?" Analyze, argue, educate the desire itself.

"Well, I see the benefit from the film is not so great," it will say.

"Then why can't you wait? I will certainly oblige you sometime later, maybe tomorrow." Don't always be so adamant. It's necessary to give in a little now and then. But you can't give in for anything and everything. If something gentle is desired, give in.

It's like giving in to a little coffee once in a while. I usually advise people that coffee and tea are not too good because of the stimulants in them. But if someone feels a coffee desire in the morning, he can still give in a little. "You want coffee? All right, I'll give you some." Heat a cup of milk. Put a little coffee in it. The mind is satisfied. It had coffee.

Treat your mind like somebody who is a little naughty and wants this and that. Use your intelligence. Educate your mind. Argue with it. Don't just give in to everything. Once in a while let it run. All these are just tricks, but very useful in training the mind.

As you continue your practice you will experience different degrees of accomplishment. In Hindu scriptures, the Lord says, "Fix your mind on Me alone. Let your thoughts dwell on Me. You will hereafter live in Me alone." That's perfect Yoga and the highest form of worship. If you're not yet able to fix your mind one-pointed on God, then when the mind wavers bring it back again and again and again to Him. This is the next best practice —concentration—that leads to steady meditation. If you're not yet able to practice this, just keep doing things, but while doing them, say, "I'm doing them for You." When you get the results, at least give a little to Him.

If you can't just sit and meditate, don't despair. Get up and do something. Get into something. It's like trying to sleep. If you can't fall asleep, don't just roll around in bed. Get up and do something until you feel sleepy. Then when you go to bed you'll sleep easily.

Not everybody is interested in sitting and meditation. Many active people can't do it. That's all right. There's still a meditation for them. It's called Karma Yoga, meditation in action. Even when you're physically doing something, your aim can be meditation. After all, what is meditation? Focusing your entire mind on what you are doing. If you think of your friend or your business when you wash a dish, the dish can't be washed clean. You might leave a spot on it. So, doing one thing at a time and doing it well is a form of physical meditation.

Sitting is a mental meditation. You allow the body to relax while you sit and do everything with the mind. Sit quietly. Focus the mind on the object you have chosen, or just repeat a mantra. Do nothing else. Forget everything. To hear the inner sound, close your ears, eyes, and mouth and listen to the sound of life within. Be still physically and mentally. Be totally relaxed. Then simply look and listen for something within. Don't open your eyes, but try to feel something vibrating within you. You don't need to do anything. Instead, be completely still and watch what's happening within. You'll enjoy that.

You may combine the mantra with the breath in any way that is comfortable, either splitting the mantra sounds on the incoming and outgoing breath, or doing one repetition with the inhalation and another with the exhalation. If you watch carefully, you can feel the breath saying the mantra. Then you can stop repeating it and just listen for that. This needs the complete attention of an indrawn mind.

As the breath comes in, feel it go deep to strike at the base of the spine. Then as it comes out, feel it roll upward through the spine to the crown of the head. Don't feel the breath flowing out through the nostrils. In the beginning it might be difficult to follow the breath up and down the spine, and you will just feel it coming in and out of the body. But after a few months practice you will be able to follow the breath along the spine.

As your meditation gets deeper you can feel the breath and energy moving upward to strike at the top of the head. If you carefully observe the path along the spine, you will be able to feel a very mild heat or a gentle warmth which is very pleasant. Try not to miss that. Once you feel it, put your entire attention on it.

The purpose of following the breath is to become conscious of the psychic energy traveling along the spine, passing through the *chakras* or spiritual centers. These nerve plexuses located along the spinal column can be used as a focus for your mental gaze during meditation. However, it's inadvisable to keep the mind focused on the lower *chakras*. If you become aware of a warmth there, feel it but don't allow the mind to become fixed there. Bring the mind to one of the higher centers, such as the heart or eyebrow center. Draw the energy upward.

All the psychic nerve centers meet at a place between the eyebrows—not outside, but deep within, almost at the central part of the skull; to be precise, at the location of your pineal and pituitary glands, which are called Siva and Shakti in Yogic symbolism. They have the bull as a vehicle; the thyroid gland. Siva rides the bull, so we say he is the Commander-in-Chief, since the thyroid commands the whole system. It is a replica of the whole body itself. You may choose to focus your meditation either in the loving heart center or at the central tower between the brows which is the location of the holy of holies or *sancta sanctorum*.

Sometimes in meditation you may hear a subtle humming sound. But when you try to hear it better, it disappears. It's like a lover. If you see her, she won't see you. But if you keep on doing something, she will look at you. When you hear that hum, that's the sign of true love. The sound of the God in you loves you when you are not aware of it. It's not that you shouldn't be aware, but the moment you become aware you become a little excited or frightened and disturb the serenity out of which the hum is generated.

It's like seeing your face reflected in a large basin of water. As soon as you see the beautiful face there, you may reach for it, disturbing the calm surface and causing the reflection to disappear. Just wait patiently. Keep looking. Slowly you will begin to see the face again.

So, know what might happen in meditation. Then when it happens you won't be excited or anxious to have more, both of which disturb the mind.

You may wonder, is this really the cosmic sound I am hearing? Even if it's your imagination, there's no harm in that. Even if it's an illusion, it's better than other illusions. You are not imagining a demon, but something nice. It's good to imagine something nice. Ultimately, you become what you imagine. Until you actually see or hear something, you have to begin with imagination. Later it will come by itself—maybe a little different than you imagined it. Don't think these experiences are illusions.

To come out of meditation, slowly increase the duration of your inhalation and exhalation. Make the breath longer. Feel the air flowing out through your nostrils. Inhale and exhale deeply a few times.

17. Tantric Yoga

Many people ask if they can practice tantric Yoga when they are married. They think it has to do with sex. This is a complete misunderstanding of tantric Yoga, which doesn't involve any sexual union. The tantric scriptures of old are not referring to physical union, though they sometimes use terms of that nature to express a certain spiritual coming together.

In the Christian tradition you may say a sister is wedded to God or the church, or you can say a pious Jew is wedded to the Torah. Of course, this doesn't mean a marriage for any sexual purpose. It's the same in tantric Yoga. The union is of Siva and Shakti, which are the masculine and feminine vibrations or powers that are within each of us. The power that creates and manifests is Shakti. The static part, which is the cause or the basis, is Siva. In the body itself, the power of Siva is from the naval upward. The power of Shakti resides below.

Anything that pulls you down should be pulled up. So that subtle force—the creative energy—that may draw you into the sensory area should be raised up. In deep meditation the mind becomes still. You build up static energy—a little warmth—which is Shakti. That is slowly raised to the head, Siva, where they unite. By your regular meditation practice you awaken that great energy stored at the base of the spine, often called the *kundalini* force. It happens when your mind is one-pointed in deep meditation.

That union of Shakti and Siva is figurative. Spiritual teachings are often given in code language. Don't think everybody can read the Bible and understand it. Ancient scriptures all have that esoteric or inner meaning. Here the tantric or spiritual union is described as the union of the female aspect with the male aspect or Shakti with Siva. That language can easily be misunderstood as referring to physical union.

Some people take advantage of the language in the tantric scriptures, "I'm going to teach you tantric Yoga," they say. "Come sleep with me." With a heavy heart I tell you that some so-called gurus do this, and to them I say, "If you want to have sex, be open about it. Say, 'I love you, child, I love you, my devotee.' Do as you like, but don't bring in the scriptures pretending to be teaching something." Even devils can quote scriptures.

There's a great deal of misunderstanding about these things. If you come across a tantric Yoga book you may read of the offering of *madya* which is wine or liquor. Some will say, "You are my goddess; I am the god. Let us offer *madya*. Drink, then have sex." This is not the drink that is meant in the teachings. The *madya* are certain hormones within. Precisely, they are the subtle psychic hormones produced by the pituitary and pineal glands, and the force behind and around them. When that *kundalini* or creative force rises up, it brings warmth to those glands, and they secrete this hormone which no doctor has ever seen in his test tubes. That hormone is called *madya*, the nectar you taste when Siva and Shakti are joined in union. You become exhilarated. You are spiritually intoxicated by that nectar.

Unfortunately, this has all been misinterpreted on a worldly level. Some people are "teaching" tantric Yoga. But this very union will happen in your regular meditation. Tantric union will happen during any deep meditation, at the point when you have kept your mind still for a considerable amount of time.

It can be proven scientifically. When the body is completely motionless, you will feel a warmth. Because there's no wastage, the energy becomes static, just like the warmth of the current you feel in a condenser. You can feel a battery's warmth because there is current which isn't flowing, but is stored. During meditation you store all your *prana*, your vital energy, in the body. There's no mental movement, no disturbing thoughts arising in the mind, so even that small amount of energy used to shake the mind is saved. This builds the static energy that creates a warmth.

When you go deep into meditation for such an experience, your body must also be capable of bearing it. Otherwise it will burst, as when you try to store too much current in a weak condenser. This is why the body must be built up with Yoga practices.

So, build a pure, strong, and flexible body. Then develop this force in you. Let it build up through your deep meditation. Rouse the static power to go through the spine and ascend to the skull. That is the Meru, the Himalayas, the height, the heavens. This is the moment you taste the nectar of spiritual union and are intoxicated by that great experience.

PART III:

THE HUMAN BODY IS A TEMPLE

18. Hatha Yoga

The human body is a temple. Keep it strong and supple. Treat it gently. The codes of living, *Yama* and *Niyama*, are the first two limbs of the eight branches of Yoga. The third is *asana*—Yoga postures that purify the physical body. Never ignore the body since it is the most important instrument. Whatever you do, you need a body. That's why the ancient Yoga teachings always emphasized taking good care of the body. In almost all the great religious traditions this is indirectly said—but not as openly or with such emphasis as in Yoga.

To purify the body we practice the disciplines of Hatha Yoga —the *asanas* or postures and *pranayama* or breathing techniques —which take care of the health of the physical body. This carries over into diet too. Avoid anything that contains toxins or that unnecessarily stimulates your body—try to eliminate alcohol and tobacco. Without purity of the body it's very difficult to purify the mind.

Learn to live a natural life. First be physically at ease; mental peace will automatically follow. Live in a way that makes your body light, healthy, and more supple. Then when you sit in meditation you won't feel aches and pains, and spend all your time meditating on them. Meditation needs all these aids. You can't just eat anything you want, then go sit and meditate. The body will say, "No, I won't allow it." You need co-operation between the body and the mind. That's why you train the body in doing all kinds of Hatha postures and breathing practices. Then, when the time for meditation comes, you can meditate on whatever you like with ease. Physical ease is maintained through proper food, proper exercise, and proper air. The physical postures bring ease to the body. Tension is released and toxins are eliminated.

You can practice Hatha Yoga on your own until you get a teacher. Read any book and try it yourself. Get used to it. Later, you will find a good teacher and you can get some points corrected. But, remember—if you are using just any Yoga book, be careful. The book might say if you stand on your head for a long time, you don't have to do anything else. It's more important to learn *how* to stand upright, than to learn how to stand on your head. Don't just go right to the advanced practices. Begin easily and slowly. If you have an inflammation in the ear, bleeding gums, headache, you should not try the headstand or any upsidedown postures. I've seen many people—even healthy, normal people—who read in some book, "If you stand on your head for half an hour, you will have the golden key to heaven." So they try it for too long. When they come down they have blood clots in their eyes which take several weeks, or even months to get rid of.

When you read about it, you think you can easily stand on your head. But the headstand is not just a physical act. Your mind and body should be in proper condition to withstand the pressure. Your food should be totally different from the normal diet of most people. Your daily life should be different, dedicated, and perfectly ethical. And you should be able to preserve a great amount of *prana*, the vital energy in the breath. If your blood vessels are weak, you might get severe bleeding in the nose or ears. Without first satisfying the preliminary requirements before attempting more advanced practices, you could easily land in a hospital.

It's better to do the headstand for two minutes with ease than twenty minutes and strain the system. If you're just beginning, it's fine to do a half headstand, without lifting the legs up. Just put the head down, lift the entire trunk up but keep the toes on the floor. See how you feel. If you feel completely confident—no pain or anything—then slowly bend the legs and lift them. Don't shoot them up right away. Move along stage by stage. In fact, it's not so important to lift the legs. Just putting the body upside down brings at least 80 per cent of the benefits of the headstand. Don't risk hurting yourself. Go slowly. Judge your own capacity.

The shoulder stand is a very important posture since it tones up the thyroid gland at the base of the throat. Thyroid is like salt. No food is entirely free from salt. Even honey has a little salt in it. In the same way, the hormone produced by the thyroid goes with every other hormone as a complement to help it do some extra work. The shoulder stand is very beneficial to the thyroid gland and thus all the glands in the body. Ultimately, the shoulder stand benefits the entire body.

Women may practice Hatha Yoga postures during the menstrual period if they insist, but it's better to avoid them at that time. Still, it's all right as long as they don't strain their bodies. Practice then should be very mild and light. They shouldn't attempt any strenuous postures or strenuous breathing techniques when the body and mind are in a very relaxed state. During the menstrual period the body is overhauling its whole mechanism; all the parts are well lubricated. When you overhaul and recondition an engine, you don't put a heavy load on it. This is why during the menstrual period, anything strenuous and physically tiring, including the physical Yoga postures should be avoided.

Unfortunately this has been ignored by many people. They don't seem to know the subtle changes that are happening in the body, which if not respected, could upset the system later. In these modern times some women say, "I have to work. Every month I will be losing five days' salary. Nobody will employ me." That's your business, but nature's way is different.

If you are a beginner, don't start Yoga *asanas* during pregnancy. But if you have already been practicing at least six months before, then continue, but reduce the more strenuous positions. Do a lot of relaxing and deep breathing. A lot of walking will help too. Take simple, easily digestible nourishment. Put no toxins in the system. Take a bit more calcium. When the baby is in the womb all that you do and see and think affects the child. Have beautiful pictures of saints and sages around the room. Every thought that arises in the mother affects the baby.

If you want a spiritual child, think Yogic ideas and read spiritual books. The very thoughts will be transferred into the child.

And expect an easy delivery. The pain of delivery won't even be a pain. It should be as easy as going to the toilet. The very fear of birth brings most of the difficulties through tension. Have full faith. Many young people have now gone back to natural living and want normal delivery without anesthesia. Treat yourself gently. Know that God is sending a beautiful soul through you as His vehicle. He will take good care of it. You can practice Yoga *asanas* almost to the time of the birth.

Anyone who practices the positions should think of the *asanas* as a meditation session. Yoga means ease and one-pointedness of mind. Take it easy and have an attitude of meditation throughout the whole session. You can meditate on the different postures by noticing the feelings you get while in the postures and the benefits too. If you are practicing with other people, don't look at them. Feel you are alone. Just watch yourself.

When you are in a posture, make sure that you are not exerting yourself. If you are straining you are not doing Yoga. You're simply exerting or exercising the body. It's just physical exercise. Instead, make the postures "steady and comfortable," which is the meaning of *asana*. See that your breathing is normal during all the postures. Keep the breathing free-flowing when holding the postures; don't hold your breath. Take a rest between the positions whenever you feel at all tired. With practice you will need fewer rest periods between the poses, but always save time for deep relaxation at the very end.

Keep trying to perfect your form. It's all right to have some variations from the basic postures, but they are mainly to keep the mind from being bored with a set routine. It's better not to do too many variations. A good Hatha Yogi does fewer variations than someone less advanced; his practice has become simpler. All the basic poses should be done well before trying variations. Doing the postures "well" refers not only to form but capacity to hold the pose as well. Then, if you want to add a variation, it's all right. A full session of Hatha need not be more than an hour and fifteen minutes including a period at the end for deep relaxation, breathing practices, and a short meditation of one or two minutes.

If your time is limited, don't reduce the period of deep relaxation after the *asanas*. Nor should the breathing practices be reduced. If you must cut something, you may eliminate some of the *asanas*, but always include the shoulder stand and the fish poses; when you have learned more advanced *asanas* always include the peacock, the headstand, and the stomach lift. The idea is to start off with milder practices and gradually build up, adding more advanced ones. As your capacity increases you can eliminate the more elementary ones.

Don't worry if you don't have time to do a full Hatha session every day. You can do part one day and continue the next day where you left off, until you finish the whole session. While practicing the postures, always do a little less than your limitation; then you'll never reach your limit. As your practice improves you won't build tension while holding the postures. That's why the more advanced student doesn't need much rest between postures. He can go almost directly from one pose to the next. This capacity not to need much rest between *asanas* is one of the signs that you are advancing.

After the series of *asanas*, lie on your back and relax the entire body from feet to head. Go over the body again—mentally relaxing every part, feet to head. Then lying like a corpse, you can simply check mentally for tension. If you find tension anywhere, send a massage willing that muscle to relax. You can command your muscles and relax them at will.

19. *The Breath of Life*

When you are practicing the Hatha Yoga postures you may feel a rush of energy or *prana*. The entire system is being reorganized. You are feeling the movement of *prana* in the body. While it moves it realigns many of the parts that have been out of alignment. It's very good, and will make you more peaceful and healthier. It will never harm you.

Prana is the vital energy or force that causes movement. All movement everywhere—even the movement within the atom, even the movement of thought—is caused by *prana*, the cosmic energy. Electricity is *prana*. Your breathing is *prana*. Your digestion is *prana*. The different functions have different names, but they are all the same current or force: *prana*.

You get *prana* from food, from the sun, and from the air you breathe. It's not simply breathing. The air stops at the lungs, but the *prana* goes throughout the body. Even though your lungs may be able to convert only part of the oxygen intake for the blood, the *prana* uses the other oxygen for all parts of the body. You are a bundle of energy. This vital force is *prana*. The practice of *pranayama* leads to the control, regulation, and mastery of this vital force. It is learning to control the *prana* and direct it as you want. Oxygen is a great panacea, a fine medicine for all kinds of poisons. The world will be much happier if it knows the importance of *pranayama*.

By practicing the breathing techniques of *pranayama*, the mind becomes clear and fit for concentration. *Pranayama* purifies the nervous system and eliminates toxins from the body and blood. With *pranayama* you can eliminate the mucous in the nose which causes most hayfever and sinus discomfort. *Prana* is also the best cosmetic. One of the breathing practices is called the skull brightener. It makes your head and entire face glow with vitality from the *prana*. This is not just Yoga wisdom, it's also scientific. Today scientists know that we normally take in only 500 cubic centimeters of air in a normal breath. By using deep breathing Yoga practices we take in 3,700 cubic centimeters of air in one breath. We should all do some deep breathing now and then. Every hour do a little deep breathing.

Prana can never be polluted by anything. That's why we're still living in these cities. If the air around you is polluted, that's no excuse not to practice deep breathing. Between 4 and 6 A.M. there is no pollution. You don't even have to do anything. You will benefit by just getting up and walking around. It's also the best time to practice meditation.

You must regulate the breath for meditation because the breath binds the mind to the body. If the breath is regulated, the mind is too. Calm, slow, and steady breathing will also keep the mind very calm. But before you calm the mind through slow, steady breathing, you should become alert. In the early morning, you can reshuffle the entire system, drive off drowsiness, bring a kind of exhilaration all over the body, remove the tension from different places, and bring harmonious movement in all the cells through a specific practice called *bhastrika* or the bellows' breath.

Before meditation do three rounds of quick expulsions of the breath through the nose. Just sit relaxed but straight with nothing against your back; the chest well spread out. Take a full breath in and start sending the air out in little expulsions through the nostrils. The abdomen comes in as the air goes forcefully out of the nostrils. The breath comes in between each forceful exhalation. Ten or fifteen such quick exhalations make up one round. The last expulsion should be deeper—driving all the air out. Then take a slow breath in. Fill up the lungs and hold the breath. While holding it, bend the neck to bring the chin as close to the chest as possible in what is called the chin lock. It's like filling a balloon. You bend the neck and tie it so the air won't escape. Just hold everything there for about ten or fifteen seconds. You might feel something like a mild electric current running about. There's no danger in it, so don't get excited. Then raise the neck and very slowly exhale through the nose. Make this exhalation complete by sucking in the abdomen near the end. Take one or two normal breaths and repeat this process for a second and a third round.

This will make the body feel exhilarated and alert the mind. After this, you may beautifully prepare the mind for meditation with alternate nostril breathing, or by just slowly breathing deeply through both nostrils at the same time. Be sure to take in the maximum amount of air by expanding the stomach and the chest well as the air flows in. You may even raise the collar bone slightly at the end of the inhalation to allow more air in, but don't strain any muscles or the lungs while practicing this deep breathing. The exhalation is just the reverse. The collar bone drops, the chest empties, and then the abdomen flattens.

Patanjali says that by practice of this *pranayama* the mind becomes clear and fit for concentration. Practice a few rounds of alternate nostril breathing before meditation and you will soon experience its benefits. Breathe out slowly through the left nostril, then in through the same nostril. Then switch, breathing out through the right nostril; then breathe in through the right side. Switch again and continue in this manner.

This deep breathing is the nerve purifying breath. Continue either using the alternate nostril method or just long full breaths for at least two or three minutes. Follow the breath with the mind. Feel how it comes in, how far it goes, and how it returns. At a more advanced stage you may hold the breath for a period before exhaling. But you should work up to that very gradually or you could hurt yourself.

The main purposes of *pranayama* are to purify the system and calm and regulate the mind. Should you ever feel upset, tense, or worried, do some slow deep breathing with full attention on the breath, and you will easily bring the mind to a calm state. The *prana*—here as the movement of the breath—and the movement of the mind go together. They're interdependent. If you regulate the *prana*, you have regulated, through the movement of the breath, that same pranic movement in the mind.

If you can control the mind you are the master. *Pranayama* helps you control certain parts of the body—certain muscles which are not normally under our control. By these practices we can thus control the mind. By controlling the breath you can control that subtle *prana*. But go slow. Be patient. *Pranayama* should never be done in a hurry, nor should you try to advance too quickly because you are dealing with vital energy. The Yoga scriptures personified *prana* as a deadly cobra. So remember, you are playing with a cobra. If you play well and make the cobra dance well, you will accrue many benefits, as did the snake charmers in India. They used their snakes for their livelihood. But if they didn't play properly, they would be killed. In the same way, with *prana*, you should be very careful. Do everything gently; avoid even the slightest strain and never hurry.

During *pranayama* practices concentration should be inward to observe what is happening. On the inhalation and the exhalation concentrate on the flow of the breath. During retention, just look within and see what is happening. For each person it will be different.

On the tree of Yoga practice, the fourth limb is *pranayama*. Only a strong person can realize God. A spiritual person should be strong—not just mentally but physically too. Thus, one should learn to regulate and store vitality. *Prana* is wasted in many, many ways, such as overeating, oversleeping, overtalking, and overindulgence in sex. The Yoga sages have measured how much vitality is wasted by different actions. They know exactly how much you waste if you talk too much, if you run too much, or eat too much. They measure this according to the length or shortness of the breath.

The maximum amount wasted is caused by unlimited sex. For this reason sexual moderation is very important. Without *prana* you are both physically and mentally weak. If you want to build up your body and mind, save that *prana*—the vital fluid. It's just like oxygen which can be condensed and made into a liquid. In the same way, your seminal fluid is liquid *prana*. It is stored in the body. When it is necessary, it evaporates into a gas—*prana*—giving vitality to the body. *Pranayama* is practiced mainly to build this vitality.

How many of us are conscious of how we breathe? It just goes in and out fifteen or sixteen times each minute. Isn't it strange to see the air remaining in this holy city—the human body? How many holes does it have? In a tube with many holes or punctures the air escapes. But here we have the nine gates of the city. Yet the life breath seems to be staying. It goes out, but some power seems to be pushing it back into us. Even though we don't worry about our life breath, somebody seems to be interested that we should stay alive.

Sometimes it seems as though there is a fight between that unseen power and the breath itself. The breath complains, "What is this? You are pushing me to go in, and every time I do, that fellow destroys me. The minute I go in, he burns me and pushes me out as carbon dioxide." Isn't it so? The breath comes in with life, and we kill it; we burn it. The air may not want to come again, but the Force says, "No, this is My baby. I have to use him for a certain purpose. I have to work through him so I want to let him survive for some more time. When his work is over I will say, 'You don't have to go in there anymore.' They'll put him in a box. Until then, I have to keep him alive. Go back in."

That's why we are living. We cannot take credit for our living ourselves. We do all kinds of things to destroy ourselves, yet still we live. Isn't it surprising? We should have died long, long ago. What makes us live then? Probably He still has something to do with us.

20. *How to Stop Smoking*

If you are a smoker, remember your first cigarette. Did you enjoy it? Your lungs have adapted to nicotine, which is a completely foreign matter—poison! Yet you love it now. Your body can adapt to pain, heat, anything. The first time a young girl goes into the kitchen to cook something, she might find it difficult to pick up the kettle without a big towel to protect her hands. After a few years she picks it up with her bare hands, which became accustomed to the heat.

The human system is wonderful. That's why we are grateful to God who made our body to adapt to the environment. But that doesn't mean everything that we adapt to is good for us. We can get used to anything—even poison. I know a person who started eating nux vomica, a type of poison that he gradually stored in his body. Then he would go to play with the cobra. When the cobras bit him, they died and he survived. His poison went into the body of the cobra. Little by little you can saturate the body; it will accept anything and everything. It's not so difficult, but it's not necessarily good, because such poisons leave aftereffects in the body.

It's no surprise that we get into these habits. Look at all the advertisements for smoking and drinking. Prevention is better than cure, but we don't seem to prevent things. We seem to allow things to happen, then call for a cure. On one side, all the pictures are calling: "Come on, pleasant, cool, beautiful. Enjoy the smoke." On the other side: "Give us enough money for cancer research." We go begging to cure cancer, and at the same time spend money to make people smoke more.

On one side: "Drink this whiskey. Get intoxicated. It's beautiful." On the other side, "You are drunk, and caused this accident. You murdered this man. Go to prison." What kind of law is this? Is it fair? Why do you allow the advertisements for smoking and alcohol, then put the offender in jail? Probably because the people who pass the laws also like to smoke and drink themselves. The so-called refined, tip-top grown-ups go for tranquilizers, sleeping pills, or nice extra-long cigarettes. The modern younger generation goes for cheaper stuff—grass, and LSD—which in the end isn't any cheaper. And those "refined" smokers call the unrefined smokers barbarians and put them in jail. Why not put everyone who smokes in jail—not just the grass smokers but also those who use the extra-long cigarettes? Why leave them to ruin their lives? Of course you can't make laws against this. The more laws you make, the more people break them. You can never achieve anything by forcing anybody. But by education you can change things.

You can't get your tranquility in a drug store or with sleeping pills. Tranquilizers can never give you real tranquility. Sleeping pills can never give you real sleep. Cosmetics will never make you beautiful. Real beauty and tranquility are based on a peaceful mind. It's the mental ups and downs that bring the furrows. The face that is naturally beautiful becomes disturbed and wrinkled because of a disturbed mind. You don't need a cosmetic to make yourself beautiful. You don't need pills for sleep or tranquility. You don't need alcohol or drugs to get yourself high.

People today worry about air pollution, but they don't worry about pollution inside. Very often I see people arguing about pollution with cigars in their mouths. They don't realize they are polluting their own lungs while talking about pollution outside. The solution to pollution begins at home. It's polluted people who bring more pollution. The cause of pollution is within. The cause of hatred is within. The cause of war is within. Man's mind is the cause of everything. Don't look outside to find the culprit. Don't blame the other man. It's the mind that creates all the wars. And it's the mind that can make the whole world a heaven.

We are in the world to grow mentally, to gain more experience, to realize the truth. The body is only a vehicle. Yet the body is an expression of the mind. To have the mind calm and serene, we must take care of the physical body. We should purify the body to help realize the peaceful mind. We must take care of our food, our liquids, and the air we breathe. Watch all our intakes. I am not recommending against the high you may feel from some of these intoxicants. If they would always let you be high, that would be fine. But unfortunately, they all leave aftereffects in your body and mind. Nicotine, alcohol, marijuana, caffeine, pills—they're all artificial. The effects are temporary and they leave aftereffects that throw you down even lower than before.

No one insists that you stop smoking or drinking to be a Yogi. If you can, it's helpful for you. But you might say, "I am used to that. I can't stop anymore. What can I do?" I never simply say, "Stop. Don't do this or that." If you feel you must continue, I say, "Okay. Continue what you have been doing and at the same time do something different also. The other will go away."

Instead of nicotine, what is the right thing? Smoke, but whenever you aren't smoking take deep breaths, *pranayama*. Do the breathing exercises and some physical postures. The *asanas* eliminate all the toxins. If you regularly do the Yoga postures, all these things will be easily eliminated. And by doing proper breathing exercises, you clean the lungs. You remove all the nicotine that is already inside. That is what causes the craving—the nicotine lodged inside from your earlier smoking. The practices clear away those toxins, including the nicotine. So you lose the craving. Then you won't even enjoy cigarettes anymore.

You don't need to quit smoking. Smoking will quit you if you keep practicing Hatha Yoga *asanas* and *pranayama*. Yoga is guaranteed to get you off addictions, even heroin. Many people have been helped to lose drug addictions completely with Yoga practices.

If you really want to stop smoking, first stop and analyze who wants to smoke and who doesn't. There are two entities. You don't want to smoke, but the one who wants to smoke is the nicotine already in you that craves some more. With Hatha Yoga you can eliminate the nicotine. By practicing bellows breathing you can burn it out. Through good care of your diet you can reduce the craving. If you are a strict vegetarian, you won't have that much craving. Have you ever noticed that when you eat meat, you crave a cigarette? Meat has purine in it. Cigarettes have nicotine in them and there's another INE sister, caffeine. They all go together. They like each other. That's why when you eat a nice big meat lunch you need hot black coffee and a long cigarette. There's a beauty in their unity, but it's not good for you.

If you are interested in eliminating the nicotine, at least temporarily, avoid those other two substances—or they will call for the nicotine again. No coffee, no tea, no meat. Then flush your system with a lot of liquids. Take nice hot baths or saunas. Let the body perspire a lot. See that you urinate a lot, and that there is no constipation in your system. Let all the elimination processes be free.

You can easily eliminate the nicotine in three days, one week, ten days at the most. It depends how much nicotine you stored and how much you are eliminating. Once that goes away, you are free from nicotine and you will see the craving gone. I have seen many, many people who through this method were able to stop smoking. You have to hold on for a few days to get rid of the nicotine. Then, even if somebody pushes a cigarette in your mouth, you won't enjoy it anymore. You'll say, "I don't need it."

In addition to all this, convince your mind of the gain. Know that the lungs are not made for nicotine, but for oxygen. God has created your lungs. He has given oxygen free to you. If He wanted you to have a little nicotine, it would not have been very difficult for Him to have added a dose of nicotine in the air itself —free.

21. *Food Makes the Mind*

Diet plays a very, very important part in people's lives. Food not only makes the body, it makes the mind. It has a direct connection to the attitudes of the mind.

If you want to see this for yourself, go to the zoo and look at the animals. Note the differences in their natures. All the carniverous animals are caged. Even within the cage they cannot easily stay quiet.

All you see is their restlessness, their constant pacing. Even after ten years the tiger is still poking his nose through the bars. Restlessness of the mind is caused by the diet. Even their excretia is foul smelling because the meat diet produces a lot of toxins. Of course the animals have the capacity to eliminate that. They just take what they want and the rest of the toxins are eliminated. In the elimination you can see the decayed matter coming out, so the smell is foul.

Then look at the herbivorous animals. They are soft, gentle, yet strong. The cow, the goat, the horse—even the elephant. Look at their excretia, no foul smell at all in either the urine or the stool. In India they use cow dung to clean the floor because it's not foul smelling. Watch the cow, see how meditative she is, how gentle. They are such peaceful animals. Where does that peace come from? Mainly their diet.

Look at the construction of the animals' bodies. The herbivorous animals have flat teeth, soft tongues, and hooves. The carnivorous animals have hooked teeth to tear the flesh, claws and rough tongues to take the flesh from the bones. Besides that, to catch their prey, they can see at night. Eyes, tongue, teeth, claws—these are the visible indications. To which category does man belong? You can decide for yourself. We don't have claws, so we make forks. We have flat teeth, we don't have a rough tongue, and we can't see at night. We can't digest the meat, so we have to cook it. Man's constitution is not meant for meat. Many doctors today agree that meat has animal fat which leaves purine in our bodies. That, in turn, converts into cholesterol. This is all known today. But if the tongue wants it, we can find many excuses to take it.

If you can, avoid all flesh foods and animal fats—including eggs, which also have that flesh part in them. When you break an egg, it decays, giving off a foul smell. Dairy products do have some animal fats in them. If you want to be a strict vegetarian you need not even take dairy products. But they have a different quality. Milk is not meat. Someone might say to you, "The milk comes out of the cow. If you drink the milk, why don't you eat the cow's flesh?" You can reply, "When you were a small baby didn't you take milk from your mama? You did, but would you cut the flesh of your mama to eat?" It's simple enough. There's no need to have lengthy discussions about this. Milk is different from flesh. We take milk from the mother and not the flesh. So we take milk from the cow and not the flesh. Milk has a special quality. It's a very *sattvic* food. It doesn't have that concentrated fat found in meat.

Of course, if we drink too much milk, it will leave a kind of phlegm, since we can't digest it well. Otherwise, it only has a limited amount of fat. Milk is a whole food. Children grow with milk alone. But after some time we do not need milk. We can live on raw fruits, nuts, and vegetables. The food we eat should be easily digestible and leave no toxins in the body. Vegetables, grains, nuts, and fruit are free from disease-producing germs.

Just look at our great-grandfathers; the four-legged ones from whom we came, according to Darwin. I mean the monkeys. They eat nuts, fruits, leaves. See how vigorous they are. They get everything they need from such a diet. They are strong animals with great vitality.

Some people still want animal flesh because they are worried about getting enough protein. No doubt meat has a lot of protein. But did you ever test it in a lab to find out all the facts and figures? I'm simply speaking from my own experience. I've been eating only vegetarian food all my life. I'm very healthy and strong. You don't need as much protein as is in the animal. It's too concentrated. The human body needs a milder form of protein which can be easily assimilated without much cooking. Instead of eating the animals which eat the vegetables, why not take the protein directly from nature yourself? Even when you want to eat animals, you choose the ones who eat vegetables. You don't want an animal that eats another animal.

We *can* get the protein from vegetables—mainly from lentils and soybeans, sunflower seeds, sesame seeds, wheat germ, yeast powder, cheese, milk, and many types of nuts. The human body is made for vegetable food, not for animal food.

As Yogies we want to cause as little pain to other beings as possible. It is easy to rationalize if our tongues desire to eat animals. We might argue, "Plants have consciousness." They do, no doubt, and some scientific experiments have proved this. We probably hurt them somewhat when we take them for eating. But there are subtle aspects to consider. The difference between vegetables, animals, and man is in the expansion of consciousness. There is consciousness in a tree, but it is more or less like dreaming. In a stone there is consciousness too. It is like sleeping. Everything has consciousness. But the degree of expanded consciousness varies. In human beings consciousness is the most expressed or expanded and has the most feeling. Whatever has the more expressed or expanded consciousness is more sensitive—even the slightest touch will be felt.

This sensitivity varies even among human beings. Imagine a classroom of forty students. Two of the boys are being mischievous when the teacher walks in. One is the most brilliant student; the other, extremely dull. "You fools," he calls. "What are you doing?" Will his scolding them hurt their feelings? Yes. But whose mind will be hurt more? You don't need to be a philosopher or psychologist to answer. On a simple level, the very bright boy will be more sensitive to the harsh words of the teacher. The other might even laugh: "Ha. He called me a fool. He is interested in me." He may even be proud because the teacher seldom speaks to him. He might be happy to have gained attention. But the brighter student may not sleep for a few nights because he is so hurt.

This is the development of intelligence and the expansion of consciousness. The more developed one is, the more one feels. You are more likely to kill an animal than a human being because you know that the human being feels more than the animal. In the same way, the feelings of vegetables are much less evolved than the feelings of animals. If to eat we must hurt something, at least let us hurt that which will not feel it so greatly.

Here is the point: Aim at the least pain whenever possible, even among the fruits on the same tree. Go to the apple tree and try to pick its fruits. One apple doesn't come easily. You have to use force because it's not yet mature. But the minute you touch the other apple, it falls right into your palm. Taking which fruit hurts the tree less? When you take the ripe fruit, you probably make the tree happy. It's ready to give and you are accepting. The other fruit says, "Don't pick me. I'm not ready." If you do it by force, it hurts. If you are conscious of not causing hurt, even such subtle differences as these can be noted.

If food comes to you very easily, you may eat it. If it draws away or runs from you, don't take it. When you kill an animal and it cries, it is not ready to be eaten by you. You might believe that animals were created to serve human beings. Probably the animals were not told this, or they didn't read the scriptures. It is man who expects the animals to serve him. Using animals for your benefit doesn't always mean eating them. If you feed them well, you can milk the cow, plow the land with the bull, and pull a cart with or ride the horse.

I always say to people who still want to eat meat, "It's fine, but don't buy the meat. Go kill him yourself. Then eat." Let me see how many people will eat meat then. If you have to kill it yourself, you see all the blood and excretia rushing out, the animals crying and yelling when you kill them. Will you eat them then? You eat them only because someone else does all the killing, and it just comes nicely to your dining table. But the one with a tender heart, can't do that. You can't kill any animals if you have a loving heart.

Of course I wouldn't preach this to the Eskimos in Alaska. There you will die if you eat only vegetables. If there is truly a need, you must eat the animal. It's all right to survive. If nothing else is available, don't you sometimes hear of people eating their own kind? When nothing else is available don't be surprised if you see people turning to cannibalism. Should I come suggesting a vegetarian diet at a time like that? "Don't eat this. Don't eat that." Use common sense. But when foods that are good for the body and the mind are available, of course take them.

Even when you travel, it's not hard to avoid eating flesh food. Just ask for a sandwich or a raw salad. It's always there. Cheese is always available, or just bread and butter. In the United States you can get the best vegetarian food—maybe better than in India.

If you have guests or parents who visit and you know they prefer meat, what should you do? Such problems occur in our daily life. Sometimes one partner in a married couple prefers not to eat meat and the other wants it. Each should think of the other. The one who makes the meal with joy should prepare meat for the other or the guests and serve it without making a sour face. That's a great achievement and a great quality. Still, *you* can eat as you prefer. But these things are very personal. You should not insist that the other person follow what you like. If you are really interested in slowly converting someone to a better diet, set a good example. Whoever he falls sick he may wonder at your health and ask your advice. Then you can gently suggest a healthier diet. Your words will then have more power.

22. *How to Eat*

Endlessly bountiful, Om, beloved Mother Nature,
Who gives food to all,
May I partake of Your food,
To gain wisdom, dispassion, attainment, and health,
To find permanent peace and joy.

The entire Nature is my mother;
The Lord of all is my father;
All the peoples are my relatives;
The entire universe is my home.

May this be an offering to that truth
Which is God.
May the entire creation be filled with peace and joy.

Do you understand this prayer? I often say this before I eat.
"Grant us health, wisdom, strength and dispassion." Why do we
want to eat? We are requesting Mother Nature to give of herself
to us. What we want is not just strength to develop our biceps
and triceps in order to break the bones of another person. We
are seeking discriminating wisdom and dispassion, which are the
two things we need to make our journey purposeful and easy. So
everyday when we eat, we say to that expression of God that is
Mother Nature, "It is for this purpose I am begging your food.
Increase the *sattvic* tendency of my mind. Give me of Yourself so
that I may get these benefits."

Know when you eat that all food is God's body. Your eating should be a sacrifice. When you eat, you should think, "I am eating to gather energy, the better to serve others." Whatever you eat, offer it to God and see the Lord in it.

Do not accept food from just anybody. Take or eat only from known hands. Never eat when you are tired, in a hurry, or angry. For mental peace continually sacrifice or give of yourself. For physical peace, have the right food at the right time in the right quantities and with right thinking while you eat. If you think angry or unhappy thoughts when you eat, the food will be poison. Think why you are eating. If you like, you can even be mentally chewing a mantra while you chew the food.

Always look for the most natural foods. If possible raise your own vegetables organically. Natural food is the best food. We don't always have to pay to eat. Like a baby sucking the milk from the mother, we too can suck from Mother Nature, taking from the ground the potatoes and all the natural food we have planted and harvested ourselves. Too often we pay not only for the food we buy, but for the efforts of others who bring food to the door of the store. Then we run to some club to exercise for better digestion and to lose the extra weight.

If, instead, we ourselves put in the effort to plant and grow the food, we will have plenty of exercise to go with the food itself. Then we don't need health clubs. How many people won't even pick up a broom and clean their own houses? Yet they pay a lot of money for memberships to work off the calories at the club.

Today many businesses offering to help you reduce are just a racket. Weight-reduction books, weight-reduction recipes, weight-reduction corporations! It's real nonsense. What's the harm in having a few extra pounds? As long as you don't fall sick, it's all right to be a little heavier than the average. If you feel healthy, you don't need to reduce to become slim like someone else. We are not all built the same way. Why should we look the same? We should just accept what and who we are. We don't have to imitate others. Remember a deer is a deer, and an elephant is an elephant. Some vegetables are slim like string beans, others are plump as pumpkins. Both are vegetables. Should the pumpkin want to imitate the string bean? Be who you are and don't worry constantly when you eat or drink.

But if you're certain your extra weight is not good for your health, there are means to change some of your eating habits. Keep practicing your Yoga postures. Eat anything you want but begin to limit your quantities. And don't become manic about being overweight. That mental agony will affect your digestion. "Oh, I am eating so much, I don't know what will become of me." That fear affects digestion, causing fermentation in your system. You should just eat happily thinking, "God has given this to me. I am eating it and I am going to digest it well." The confidence must be there.

If you eat well and digest well, you won't have that false hunger which now and then arises between meals. If hunger is real, you don't have to curb your appetite. But sometimes the appetite is false. Watch out for habitual hunger. Don't just eat because something is delicious or because it's twelve o'clock. Eat when you're really hungry. Even then, don't simply eat anything and everything. Learn to eat the right foods—clean, plain food, not mixed with too many other foods, not too spicy or filled with stimulants. You are eating for your mind and for your body, not for your tongue. The food should be plain, tasty, and easily digestible.

Before you respond to hunger, ask yourself carefully, "Who wants to eat now—the tongue or the tummy?" Then wait. If your stomach is really hungry you cannot just put the appetite aside. But if it's temporary or habitual hunger, and you engage yourself in doing something, the hunger will go away. Then when you finally do eat, eat well. Don't try to cut back then. Eat until you are satisfied.

Everything you take into your body should nourish you. Don't let the food be too spicy because that will disturb the mind—and even affect dreams later. Some liquids—water, milk, fruit juices —don't disturb the body. But strong black coffee or tea kindles up the system because of the caffeine going into the blood stream. Alcohol is even worse. Anything that is fermented becomes alcohol. That fermentation is an acid. Alcohol is used very well to preserve dead bodies, but it's not for the living. Be careful what you put into your body.

Even healthy food taken in the wrong amounts won't digest and will ferment inside you. Imagine the stomach as a big oven which houses your digestive fires. You should eat according to the hunger or the gastric fire in the stomach. If you do, you'll never have any problems with food. If, for example, you eat too many foods from roots, which are starchy foods, the fire inside goes down quickly. In other words, it takes longer to digest. Fruits and vegetables, on the other hand, digest more easily.

Still, it's difficult to categorize everything. Each fire house is different. Not all people have the same amount of hunger or the same amount of digestive fire. Just because a label may say, "This is good, and contains so much protein, so take it," don't immediately buy it. You may not be able to digest that amount of protein.

Prescribe the correct diet for your stomach, not for your height or weight. You decide what is best. Watch the reactions of your stomach to each food and see how each agrees with you. If by chance it doesn't agree, stay away from it, or lessen the amount. Become your own dietician. Books can give you general guidance, but ultimately you are the best doctor for yourself.

You can overhaul your own system. Nothing will create mucous in your system if it is well digested. Otherwise, even the so-called mucous-free diet will still leave mucous to clog you up. Anything left undigested in the stomach begins to ferment. The stomach is like an airtight chamber. If you put the fruit of the vine in an airtight bottle it begins to ferment and become wine —alcohol. If you allow food to stay in the stomach a long time instead of digesting it, it ferments and becomes acid. It becomes mucous and gives gas. That means you should eat only when you are really hungry, and just to your limit. Then you can digest anything and everything. If your digestion is a little weak, you will have to look for a proper diet that will have less mucous-producing tendencies. This is another reason to avoid meat, which must be cooked a long time, and even then it won't digest easily and will leave mucous. You can eat vegetables raw, or just steam them a few minutes. Even among vegetables there are certain mucous-producing types that have more water in them— cucumbers and melons for example. Naturally, when you eat them they cool the system somewhat, lowering the digestive fire.

You can prevent gas just by studying the book of nature. For me the best book is the cow. I watch her and see how she eats, masticates, and digests. Your own stomach will tell you how long a food takes to digest. If the gastric fire is not ready when the food comes, digestion is delayed and the food ferments, producing gas and mucous. These two more or less go together. The only thing to do when you feel gaseous is not eat. If you eat the right quantity, you will digest it well and there won't be any gas. Also, if you wait to eat until you feel the real hunger, you won't have any gas or mucous problem.

If you want to help digest food, you may sit on the backs of your legs or calves in the Diamond pose. You seldom see overweight Japanese women, because many of them often sit this way, which automatically helps digestion. Another digestive aid is leaning to one side which will affect the flow of the breath. While kneeling on the floor, lean to the left, which will quickly make the breath flow through the right nostril aiding digestion.

You can prevent almost all illnesses by being attentive to your diet and by limiting the amount you eat. Any doctor will tell you that when people have little food, they are healthier. Too much eating creates a problem. We have so much abundance today that sick people and hospitals are in abundance. There are a lot of mental problems, lots of psychiatrists, and lots of insane asylums. Is that what we call a modern country?

Beyond limitation even nectar becomes poison. We grow healthier with moderate eating. Since children are growing, their bodies need much more. But if an adult or a middle-aged person is doing mostly sedentary work, he should not eat more than one full meal each day. That way he can keep his health and body in good shape. Other times, he can take some juices or a hot beverage. Of course, a manual laborer doing a full day of physical work may take solid food three times a day or even more. It's not how much you eat that is important, but how much you can digest and assimilate. If you assimilate only a portion of the food you eat, all the rest must be thrown out, which drains your energy.

The food taken should be adjusted according to the work you are doing. For mental work liquid nourishment serves best; only one solid meal a day is needed. For physical work, take as much solid food as can be assimilated. I am the proof. For the past many years I have been living on just one meal each day. And that one meal is a kind of half meal—what you would probably call a snack. Yet I seem to work quite a bit and I don't seem to get tired. The tired feeling comes from the mind—not because you are eating too lightly. If you could always keep your mind free and relaxed, enjoy what you're doing, and not be disturbed, anxious, or worried about your life or your actions, you wouldn't be tense and you wouldn't get tired. You wouldn't waste your energy, and just a little food would be enough. You can test yourself. Try eating more lightly and just see how wonderful you feel.

People sometimes ask the best way to combine foods. I'm not interested in a "balanced diet." I prefer the "monodiet." Don't put too many food varieties in the stomach at the same time. The stomach will digest better if it has just one type of food there. You might ask, "Then how do I get the other necessary ingredients?" I believe the system itself has the capacity to convert that one food into many ingredients. "Where did you learn that, Swami? Who is your authority?" The cow is my textbook and God is the authority who wrote the book *Cow*. I asked the cow, "Hey, do you eat a balanced diet?" She just looked at me and laughed, "I eat only grass, yet I am able to produce milk that contains all the vitamins."

If the cow is able to do this, I think you can do so even better than the cow. You must have that capacity. If you want to have different foods in a meal, it's all right; but be simple—not too many at once. The fewer the better.

If the food is natural, all the vitamins are there. If the food itself lacks the vitamins because of the conditions under which it was grown or processed, then you may feel the need to take a vitamin supplement. But don't take too much, or you will only be consuming money. The excess will be thrown out. I think the benefit is a psychological feeling at best. Many people think they can cure a cold by just taking vitamin C. But now the doctors say the vitamin C didn't cure the cold. It was the feeling or the belief that effected the cure, "Ah, I took vitamin C. Now I'll be cured."

You can cure yourself. Stay away from too much starch or sugar. Though fruit seems to have a lot of sweetness, it's easily assimilated. You don't have to be frightened of sugar, or stay completely away from it. Have a little bit of honey if you like. It's a natural form of glucose. It's completely different from the sugar you buy or find in most sweets. Dates are good, too, for satisfying your sweet tooth. I'm not giving you any prescription. I'm not taking the place of a doctor to treat you. These are just my suggestions.

Avoid heavy or late dinners. Your last meal should be light and eaten at least two and a half hours before going to bed. Then you'll sleep beautifully and easily waken very early.

Every time you eat something, rinse your mouth with plenty of water soon after the meal. Rinse it out at least six or seven times. Even massage the gums with the fingers while you are rinsing: you'll have no more dental problems.

In the early morning before meditation some people feel the need for a pick-me-up. You don't always have to take coffee or tea. Pero is one of the good commercial coffee substitutes. Mint tea is good too. Or roast coriander with pieces of fresh ginger root. Coriander smells good and has a good flavor. Dry or fresh ginger with a little honey also cuts mucous. Dry roast a few small pieces of ginger, add coriander seeds, and crush them in the blender; then take one or two teaspoons of this mixture, boil and strain it, add a little milk and honey, and you'll get the same pep up as you would from coffee.

You don't have to be a fanatic with your diet. If a little regular tea helps you meditate well, it doesn't matter if you drink some once in a while. Good meditation is more important than which tea you drink. But be careful of the quality of your sleep which depends on what you ate for dinner the previous night.

Our bodies and minds are very easily affected or dirtied by what we take into them. How does anything, even a room get dirty? If you leave the doors and windows open carelessly, the dust flows in, soiling the room. In the same way, if nice things come into our bodies, we keep them clean. So take care of your intake, physical and mental. Check carefully before anything comes in.

Every country has immigration offices at ports of entry. Before somebody walks in, "Hey, who are you, friend or foe? Good or bad? What are your credentials? Show me your passport?" If you are a good person, they say, "Okay, come on in, be our guest." If not, "Get out."

You have a country here. Your body is your country, and there are many ports of entry—every opening, every pore. You must assign immigration officers everywhere. When you see something coming, check before it arrives and affects your brain, "Who are you? What kind of a sound is that? What kind of a food is that? Oh, a good food that will make me tranquil. Okay, come on in." Otherwise, "I'm sorry, sir, but I don't need you."

That's what you call *pratyahara*, or sense control, which is the fifth limb on the tree of Yoga. Have a check on your senses. Have tongue control. If you have been feeling a bit gaseous, for example, and your friend brings you a delicious piece of apple pie, don't forget your stomach and take it. How easy to forget when the eyes see the pie and the tongue calls for it. Always question whether the stomach wants it or not. You cannot simply overwork one fellow down there for the pleasure of the others. If you give a secretary too much to do before she has finished the earlier jobs, she will grow disgusted and quit. If you keep on overworking the stomach, he will go on a strike.

23. Fasting

Fasting allows you to eliminate toxins from your system. When you fast, anything that's not good for your system is cast out, because the energy in your body that is normally used to digest your food is used for this elimination.

You must know how long you need to fast in order to remove all the toxins in your system. Allow just enough time to eliminate all the toxins. During the period of the fast, you may drink as much water as you like, which flushes the system just like flushing out a radiator in your car. But if you feel a little weak and can't sustain yourself on water alone, there's no harm in drinking apple juice or grape juice. You can still eliminate toxins by drinking fruit juices for strength. Fresh juice is much better than canned juice which probably has a little acidity in it.

When you fast you are reconditioning your body almost as you would overhaul a machine. Every part of your body will become delicate and more sensitive after the fast. The duration of the fast depends on how much toxin you have in you. After these have passed out of your system your tongue will be clean and you will know you've fasted long enough. The elimination may come in various forms: small pimples, boils, abscesses, perspiration, and many other ways. Don't be frustrated or frightened if this happens. You might even feel a little itchy. If you do, avoid salt and try not to scratch yourself or you will just continue to itch.

During the first one or two days of the fast you may not feel anything at all. The third day you might feel a little weak. The tongue will suddenly become coated. Your breath might have been smelling all right until then, but then its odor becomes foul and your saliva tastes salty. Your perspiration also has a bad odor. All this odor and coating are coming from within. It's a good sign. It means everything is being thrown out. You have to wait a little longer. You might experience headaches, even nausea and vomiting. These are not uncommon when fasting.

People often say, "Whenever I stop eating, I get nauseous. I get a headache. I better eat." These are common symptoms; you have to wait a little longer. To eliminate toxins more quickly, drink plenty of water to help flush them out; take showers; do deep breathing. It all takes time: three or four days, sometimes even five. Slowly the coating on the tongue will go away. Your eyesight will be improved and you will feel light. All your aches and pains will go away. Each of your senses becomes more sensitive. Your saliva will become tastier—even sweeter than 7-Up. Most people have not tasted their own pure saliva. Their tongues are coated, their taste buds have lost their capacity to taste, and their saliva is filled with toxins.

As the fast continues you will experience these healthy symptoms. Your body will feel so light you can walk much faster, as if you are flying. The Palani Temple in southern India is at the top of a hill with about 1,500 steps leading to it. I used to attend the sunrise and evening services every day. Once I fasted for fifty-one days and I had to climb up and come back to my room twice each day. For the first two or three days I couldn't do it. But as the days passed, I felt like jumping four or five steps at a time. I felt like I was flying. I just couldn't go one step at a time, because I felt so light.

When you begin to get those good signs, you can prepare to stop your fast. After a long fast the real hunger comes; you can't ignore it because it will eat at your flesh. When that real hunger comes don't starve yourself. When you feel your senses are alert and you are really hungry, begin to eat something.

Breaking the fast is even more important than the fast itself. After the fast don't feast or pounce on a big meal; you can seriously harm yourself. Break it with something very light. If you don't have the patience to break the fast slowly, don't fast.

Your body is something like a totally reconditioned car engine. You can't run it immediately at 100 miles per hour. You shouldn't even run it beyond 35 miles per hour. You very gradually let the engine get worked in. The body is also a machine, and by fasting you have reconditioned it. Work with it slowly after the fast.

The period of breaking the fast—before you resume normal eating—should be *equal* to the period of the fast itself. If you fast for a week, break the fast slowly for a week. To break the fast step-by-step, consider what you were taking during the fast. If you were fasting only with water, take a little fruit juice or buttermilk, though even milk is a bit heavy. The best thing is apple juice. For the second meal—or if you are on a fruit juice fast—try something semi-solid like Cream of Wheat pudding or some yogurt. Put some small pieces of cucumber in yogurt, add a little salt, a sprinkling of pepper, and some fresh coriander leaves. It's a good recipe. Or cook some cream of wheat with milk or water, and add a little honey. It's really tasty and it's not heavy. Eat just a cup at first.

See, first liquid, then semisolids. As long as you can postpone it —even to the third, fourth, or fifth meal—eat semisolid food; then some well-steamed vegetables, a piece of bread, a little cooked cous-cous, or some well-cooked rice. Postpone eating a heavy meal. Imagine that you are very carefully breaking in your new body.

But please don't then go to the other extreme. It's best to eat once a day and be a Yogi. If you eat twice a day, you can still enjoy the world and be happy. But eating three meals a day can easily send you to the hospital. Limit your life for more joy. Gradually train yourself to take the right food each day in the right amount. Then you won't need to fast for long periods to remove toxins.

In normal daily life it's good to fast one day a week, taking only water or fruit juices—no dairy products. The effect of fasting Thursday is felt on Friday. During the other days be careful in eating; don't overload your system. You will always feel light and be healthy.

The purpose of fasting is to experience good health—no more aches and pains anywhere. Your body won't bother you. When you sit and meditate you won't have physical distractions; you will simply have forgotten your body. You can then do more things with your mind. Whatever you want to do, know that the body must come first. Take care of it. Fasting is a wonderful opportunity to do that. It's a fine practice which is why many of the holy days of the great religions are often combined with one type of fast or another. There are fast days in all religions. Even if you don't fast for a spiritual or religious reason, doing so just for the sake of your health is very good. Even if you don't have time for a long fast, fasting one day each week will certainly help you.

24. Heal Yourself

You can become your own doctor. In Yoga you bring health to yourself by eating the proper food, taking enough rest, fasting to eliminate all the toxins, and doing Yoga postures, while avoiding any which might aggravate pains you have. The breathing practices are also very important. You can heal yourself with fasting and by deep breathing and by directing *prana* to the affected area.

Visualize the part where you have the ache or the pain. When you breathe in, direct your attention to the area. Feel that you are taking *prana* from outside; you are taking in beautiful vitality which is given by God through nature. Breathe in as if you are swallowing gallons and gallons of vitality. Feel that it is going directly to the place that aches. Hold your breath for a few seconds while thinking that it is going there and building up that area by removing the dead or diseased cells and tension. Then, when you breathe out, feel that you are throwing out all of the illness. It's a beautiful practice. By doing this you can cure many of the aches and pains in the body. *Prana* has that power. It can penetrate anywhere and everywhere—just through your thinking. That is the secret of Yoga practice.

Even if you miss doing the Yoga postures occasionally, don't miss the breathing practices which alone will tone up all the glands. *Prana* is the best tonic. Simple breathing can heal. Just divert that work energy to wherever you have a problem. Even if it's a long-standing illness, do a lot of *pranayama* and, when you are practicing deep breathing, just feel that you are directing the *prana* to the affected part. But never strain when you do the deep breathing. You're already breathing. Just do it a little deeper that's all.

You don't always need a lot of doctors in your life. There's an old saying, "One doctor, consultation; two doctors, prescription; three doctors, cremation." Let us each take good care of ourselves. Medical knowledge is improving all the time, and it will continue to improve, but today's medicine is no good for tomorrow. Without sacrificing any life we can still find ways to keep ourselves healthy. We don't have to torture animals to discover cures. If people just ate the right foods and led the right kind of life, there would certainly be no need for so many hospitals. Go back to nature and lead a natural life. Surely prevention is better than the cure.

I suggest natural remedies for many ills. The elements themselves can cure the body. For example, if you have pain, you can use mud packs. Hot poultices or clay packs laid against the affected area will be helpful. The earth itself has a beautiful feeling and a healing quality. Mud is nothing else but Mother Earth. When you put it on your body you are embracing Mother Earth.

Have you ever tried an oil bath? It's a complete lubrication and will remove very many ailments. Profusely apply the oil all over the body, massage yourself well, let the body soak in the oil for a half hour or so, then wash it off under a shower. Don't apply soap. Wipe away what's left with a towel. If you use sesame oil, it will take away the toxins and be very helpful for arthritis and rheumatic troubles. The fat in the sesame seed is totally different from animal fat. People who have cholesterol troubles should use sesame oil in cooking and take sesame oil baths. They can even eat sesame candy if they want. The sesame seed is miraculous.

If you still have oil on your skin after your bath, mix some chickpea powder with a little water until it makes a paste and apply it. You could also use mung bean powder mixed with water or apply yogurt. When you take a shower the excess oil will come off. You can also use the same powders to clean the hair.

The best agent of cleaning is clay. Soft clay smeared all over the body leaves the skin with a fine texture. Make a thin paste of soft clay and rub it all over the body. Allow it to dry for a couple of hours, then just wash it off. See how beautiful your skin is. All the poisons are squeezed out. Earth has the maximum capacity to draw out all the toxins.

If you have a fever, put a little soft clay soaked with water on some linen, fold the cloth, and tie it to the forehead. It reduces the temperature. If you have any inflammation, apply a mud pack the same way.

You can also heal your body just through your thinking. Every one of your thoughts has a certain power over your body. The actions of the mind are clearly visible in certain areas. Your glands change first. Isn't it true that the moment you think of a delicious candy your salivary glands act? That is how your thoughts affect your body. If you think that you are sick, you are surely going to be sick. Think that you are healthy, and you *are* healthy. Remember, you become what you think. It's simple: Think well, you become well.

Think very well, and others also become well. Yes, you can send *prana* to others. You can send a spiritual charge by your touch. If you're really charged with that *prana*, you can send it long distances by thought alone. You can even charge a material object with spiritual vibrations through a meaningful offering to God in the form of food, objects, or talismans. You may then give or send this object to others or use it yourself. Good electricity conductors, such as gold, silver, and copper are also good for charging with spiritual vibrations, or *prana*.

Healing is a divine thing. I'm not quoting anything nor must you accept what I say. There was a time at the beginning of my spiritual life when I did a lot of healing—sometimes without even seeing my patient. But at a certain point something dawned in me and said, "You shouldn't be doing any healing through your own projection. You should not think that *you* are doing anything. Let God's will act through you."

Certainly we feel sympathetic toward people who are suffering, and we must be able to help them. But when we are helping somebody, we should at least know the reason they are suffering. Suffering is a means of purgation. This doesn't mean we should ignore someone's suffering, saying simply, "Oh, that's his *karma* which he's purging. Why should I do anything?" No, we must still have a sympathetic heart. But if we want to remove suffering, we should do so indirectly, and know that this capacity comes from God.

Don't even let the person know that you are doing anything to heal him. Instead, ask him to do something to heal himself. Why should we waste our energy on him if he is not ready to undergo a little discipline? If we heal him, tomorrow he will get into the same problems that caused the suffering in the first place. He must learn what has brought the suffering. He must recognize his mistakes so he won't repeat them. If somebody comes for help from cancer which is caused by smoking but won't quit smoking, why should we treat him? The cancer will come back.

People should face their own *karma*. It's the best education. It we heal someone who has not learned his lesson, it's like a professor writing an exam for a student who hasn't studied or learned anything. There can be no real promotion. So when someone comes for help, just advise him to undergo some healthy disciplines, like *asanao* and *pranayama*, and without his knowledge, send your prayers. Then he will say, "I was advised to do certain things which I did, and I was healed." If you have helped remove his suffering, you did so indirectly. You are safe from your own ego, and his discipline has purged his own karma, so he won't have to repeat the suffering.

25. Self-mastery

You can master your own body and mind. If you achieve self-mastery, then you are the master of everything. Unfortunately, many have forgotten to exercise this mastery, and the body and mind have begun to master them. If you let them, the body, mind, and senses will enslave you. If you sit to eat and are not pleased because the meal is saltless, then the tongue is dictating that you eat more for its sake rather than for your stomach's. But you can train your senses to obey you.

To control the mind you must control the senses because the mind functions through the senses. By themselves, the senses are innocent. They can't do anything. Sometimes your eyes are wide open but you don't see anything because your mind is occupied elsewhere. It's not the eyes that see, but the mind that sees through the eyes. The mind hears through the ears and tastes through the tongue.

The fifth branch on the tree of Yoga is withdrawal of the senses from sense objects. That doesn't mean you suppress anything. Instead, you gain control over it. You use the senses as *you* want and do not allow them to use you. Through the conscious mind you send proper impressions into the sub-conscious mind to erase the old impressions or habits. That's what you call the will. Use your will.

The best way to develop this ability is to begin with small things over which you can easily take control, and build from there. Instead of suddenly saying "I'm going to fast for ten days," try one day. If you think that your tongue demands too much sugar, say, "Every Sunday I will not touch sugar." After a few weeks, add one more day. Or instead of taking four teaspoons, take two. Gradually gain mastery over your tongue.

In the same way, if you visit movies frequently, then say, "Just once a week, that's all—however great it is." You can also vow not to watch television for one day. Later go two days without television. That way you slowly win over your eyes. Begin with little things, and when you achieve them you will gain confidence. That way you can choose your own practice and gradually gain control over all your senses. It's like training a horse. You don't put a big load on the horse overnight. You add to it gradually.

Learn to control your anger also. Of course it's not wise to store your anger to the breaking point until it explodes. But if you analyze it a little, you will not allow yourself to get so angry. Everytime you become angry you activate certain glands, mainly the duodenum, causing the bile to splash into the blood stream. That's what makes the blood "boil" and the face get red. After it boils it has to cool down; this uses up red corpuscles, which is why people who are often angry lose blood quality and become nervous. Then when they become angry their whole body shakes and shivers. That person is becoming a wreck—even before affecting the one who angers him. If he is strong, the other might not even become disturbed. It's completely the loss of the angry person.

Nor can people be corrected by anger. That just makes more enemies. If someone is angry at you, show love. It's like putting water on fire. Know that you, more than anyone else, are affected by your anger. The minute you get angry, look at your face in a mirror and you will be ashamed. Drink a cold cup of water or take a cold shower. Count to a hundred. There a lot of tricks.

After controlling that anger, keep it. It may come in handy. Controlled anger is often very useful—even necessary. Someone might try to exploit you or unnecessarily try to inconvenience you. If everything else fails, you can use anger to get out of that. But until you gain that capacity, stay away from it.

As your practices continue and your faith grows, you will even overcome fear which is most important to be eradicated. Once millions of people were gathering at a religious place of pilgrimage. There was a very saintly old person who couldn't really walk that far distance to join everyone. He had a small hut somewhere on the way, but if was hundreds of miles away. The pilgrims were passing through, and he had the opportunity to see all who were going to the pilgrimage. At one point he saw a kind of peculiar figure, not a human figure, going toward the place of pilgrimage.

The saint stopped him and asked, "Hey, who are you? You look a little funny. Where are you going?"

"Oh, I'm going for the pilgrimage."

"Ah, what is your purpose?"

"Well, I have an assignment."

"Tell me, what is the assignment? What is your name?"

"I'm named Mister Cholera."

"What? You're Mister Cholera? Why are you going there?"

"I have been assigned to remove five hundred people from the face of the earth, and am taking that pilgrimage as an excuse. I'm going to fulfill my mission."

"Oh, I see. Well, if that is God's purpose, you should do it. Because people go there and forget about their sanitary conditions. They create room for that, so probably you'll have lots of disciples."

When the pilgrimage was over, everybody returned to their homes. At that time the news flashed, saying that almost fifteen hundred people had died of cholera. This saintly person was a little annoyed. "Why should one who calls himself God's messenger tell a lie? He could just as well have told me that he was going to claim fifteen hundred lives. He said only five hundred, but took a thousand more. I must watch for him and ask him this question."

So he carefully looked for him, and, of course, after a couple of days Mister Cholera passed by. The saintly man approached him. "Sir, will you please stop?"

"Yes, I know your thought. I know why you have stopped me.

But don't make me responsible for that. I did only my job; I took only five hundred."

"How dare you say that? There were fifteen hundred people who died."

"Well sir, that's due to my follower, my friend."

"Who is that friend?"

"Mister Fear. I took only five hundred. But because people heard there was cholera, the very fear of cholera killed another thousand. What can I do sir?"

It's a fact. Fear of the disease kills more people than the disease itself. So make the mind strong. After all, what is it that we are afraid of? One day we are going to die. If death comes, say, "Oh, you have come. You are going to take away this garb and get me a new one? Okay, take this and get me a new model." If you only have right understanding, there's no room for fear.

To overcome fear build up thoughts of hope, courage, and faith. Don't dwell on your troubles. Use your mantra or prayer; read scriptures. If you have faith in God you need not be frightened of anything. If He doesn't have such power, why should you go in search of Him? With that faith in the Supreme Power nothing can affect you. Once a south Indian saint saw the angel of death face to face, and told him, "Don't you know God is protecting me? You better run away quickly. If He finds you coming near me He will surely destroy you. Please run, save yourself." How could he say such a thing to death itself? Because he had tremendous faith in God. That is the strength of a devotee. So build up the body, build up the nerves, and build up the mind until your faith is so strong there is no fear at all and you are the master.

26. Walking Sticks

There's no special technique I can give you, nor can I promise you, "Come on, I'll teach you this, and you'll immediately go to heaven." All the teachings are simple, and the practices too. Nothing here is very difficult. The only difficult task is ridding yourself of old habits. They will slowly go away if you cultivate new habits. It's impossible to drive away the old habits, but you can replace them with better ones.

Imagine that we are sitting together in a dark room and we want to drive the darkness away. If we each take a stick and begin beating at the darkness, crying, "Darkness, get out, get out," we will only be beating each other in the dark. We can't beat the dark. But if one small child could bring a little candle, the darkness would just disappear.

So bring the light and at the same time the darkness will go. Don't worry about any of your undesirable habits. If you just learn to replace some of them with a few of these Yoga practices, the undesirable habits will quietly say good-by to you.

You must learn to stand on your own two feet. Yoga never asks you to run away from your troubles, but teaches you how to face life. There are two voices in you, the lower self and the higher Self. If you can learn to hear the voice of your higher Self, then you can follow what it says. You will enjoy the journey it takes you on because growing is natural, not painful. Remember, the pure Self doesn't have to become happy; it is always that way. You are doing the practices—meditation, breathing, Yoga postures, etc.—so you won't lose your peace. Your practices are not to *achieve* happiness or peace, but to stop anything from disturbing it.

One of the major obstacles is the tendency we have to blame somebody else when something goes wrong. Immediately we search for a scapegoat. "Because the road is crooked, I fell down." How quickly people file suit against the road contractor. We simply don't want to accept blame ourselves. We want the insurance companies to pay for our failures; someone else should always pay for our mistake.

It's time to believe in your *karma*. When you get into some trouble, always take the blame yourself. "I must have done something somewhere, so I am facing this. Otherwise, why should this come to me?"

You cannot avoid what's coming to you, but you can learn the proper attitude to help yourself when it comes. Such guidance is the only thing a spiritual teacher can offer you. No one can guarantee anything for you, but there are some walking sticks for a slippery road. With these methods, you can walk the road yourself. If you still have a little doubt while you're on the path, a teacher may be able to help you sometime by suggesting what to do in this or that situation.

Ultimately, however, *you* have to do it. The speed of your success depends on how sincere and fervent you are. You must practice for a long time without a break and with total interest or zeal. If you have these three qualities and you follow the practices, you will surely grow. But you can't expect real benefit that quickly. The techniques are like nicely scented soaps. Hatha Yoga, meditation, mantra repetition, *pranayama*, headstand, fasting—all are soaps. Use them to wash away the old dirt. Once you have washed away the old habits, you won't need the soap. When the road is no longer slippery, will you need a walking stick?

Most people don't come looking for such walking sticks until they've tried everything else first. They thought they might find their happiness by eating something or drinking something or inhaling something or going for some personal pleasure. But nothing seemed to satisfy them for any duration. None of those other means could eliminate their unhappiness. Finally they said, "Forget it. I've tried all that, and I'm tired of it. Those things are just trash. They're not going to help me."

Such people are spiritual seekers. Those who only read about this are not true seekers. Literacy won't help. You can read all the books in the world and be a walking library, or listen to all the tapes and be a living hi-fi tape recorder with sixteen channels. But the tape recorder knows nothing about the music it reproduces. The scholar hasn't experienced what he read. The true seeker renounces everything else and takes on the practices. He dedicates everything to maintain that peace. In time even his practices are done as Karma Yoga—not simply for his own growth, but for the benefit of all others.

It's not an easy journey, but if you understand it well and know the benefits, you will enjoy it. Yogic life is always joyous. If you don't enjoy the practice and the journey, then you are not really doing anything in the name of Yoga. But just because you are enjoying something doesn't mean you may take it lightly. If you are serious when you drive, you enjoy the road. If you are careless, you won't enjoy the trip at all. Seriousness is important, but don't become tense. When you are tense, you are not practicing with the right attitude—you haven't yet understood what you are doing. According to the Yogic approach, if you understand why you are doing something, you will do it well, and really enjoy it.

However hard, difficult, or painful something is, you can still enjoy it. Think of the people who climb to the top of Mount Everest. They risk their lives; still they enjoy it. It's serious work, but they know the benefit, the glory that will come later. Though such fame is probably temporary—not worth all that much— they are willing to undergo any hardship that comes for it.

Now look at the Yogi's goal: eternal peace and joy. However difficult the journey, you can still enjoy it. Yogis perform everything for enjoyment. The whole life is a joy for them. In fact, Yogis enjoy life because they know how to live in the world without getting caught in it.

Of course it doesn't happen overnight. In the beginning you get a little tense. You think, "I *must* do this and I *must* do that, otherwise I won't get what I am going for." So, even in the name of Yoga practices you lose the little peace you have. That happens at first. It will help if you keep this in mind: "It is for peace that I am doing everything. If the very doing itself is going to disturb my peace, either the doing is wrong or my approach is wrong."

Just do your part and let the rest take care of itself. Your own haste disturbs your practice. You must learn how to practice without any anxiety, yet at the same time with proper interest. It's like learning to play a piano. In the beginning you may not know where to put your hands or what to press. The fingers ache; the foot refuses to do its job. It takes years and years of practice. But once you have learned well, you don't even need to see the keyboard. You look around and play easily.

It's a serious business, but it's worth it. I still remember how I learned to ride a bicycle. When I thought of my legs, I forgot the handlebars. When I took hold of them I forgot the pedals. When someone passed a half mile away, I lost everything completely. But with perseverance people learn. If we keep on practicing, one day we can let go of the handlebars, stand on the seat, and ride the cycle. My point is: Do your part of the duty and the result will come by itself.

No doubt beginners will experience a sort of tension or seriousness. They fear they may be doing something wrong and wonder, "Am I getting this or not?" So there's some anxiety. It's quite natural for a beginner. You should understand that. Slowly you will get used to the practices and all anxiety will slip away.

When you decide you are really a seeker, there are many hints to make your journey easier. If you are trying to give up bad habits, ask your friends to call you now and then to encourage you. If possible live with other seekers, or correspond with them. You can also put pictures around you for right associations.

Build the mind with beautiful ideas. Build the nerves with *pranayama,* and build love with chants, psalms, or mantras. You can use Yoga practices to smooth any hectic day. Do a bit of Hatha Yoga, *pranayama,* and meditation. It's like winding your clock at the beginning and the end of the day. When you get up, you should perform your spiritual practices. Begin each day with the words of a great saint or prophet. Before you practice, pray for help; use your mantra and have faith in your teacher.

Mantra repetition is the simplest method of concentration. It's always in your heart, even in the midst of your daily work. When you drive you can repeat your mantra; you can do so when you cook and even when you eat. It's very simple, and because it's dealing directly with sound, it's very subtle too. It's best not to repeat the mantra in a hurry—go slow to get the vibrations.

Remember, a little Yoga every day is better than a lot of Yoga once in a while. Read from the scriptures daily and for a while ponder the points you read, trying to assimilate them into your life.

Before you go to bed, you can say as a prayer: "Let me grow," or, if you've grown, "Thank you for the opportunity to grow a little." You may also pray for the liberation of the self from the ego shell. For a long time I used to say each night: "Every day I'm getting better."

Until you reach the level you are aiming for, you have to work hard. But even in the intensity, enjoy yourself. Be playful and relax. Never be adamant in training the heart. Know your capacity. Don't try to compete with others. If someone sitting next to you can bury his face between his knees in a forward bend, and you can't even touch your toes, are you going to break your spine? He can do that much because his body is flexible. Your body is a little stiffer. There's no competition. Go to your capacity; take it easy.

Yoga should be a joyful celebration, remember that. All your practices can be joyful celebration. So take it easy, but don't be lazy. It's very important to find the golden medium. Use your common sense. There's no hard-and-fast rule about these things. If there is one common rule for all practices, it's this: Go to your capacity, but never overdo.

The best is always the easiest. Truth is plain and should be approached with all ease. By following all these precepts and practices you will come to experience the Absolute, Supreme Truth. By practicing all the different methods, emphasizing most the ones that suit you, and by beginning from where you are, you will be refining yourself. At a certain point it will appear that you are losing your individual self completely. You become so thin—in a sense—that it is as if you are just fasting and fasting until you have eliminated everything. A point comes where there is nothing else, except that "you are." That's when you say: "I am. That's all. I am not this or that; I am. Just I."

Don't misunderstand and think you have to isolate yourself from the world to realize this. You are liberating your mind from associations, but you need not give up all your friends or neglect or ignore anyone. No, it is simply understanding that you are just you; you are not this or that. You may still have many things, but you are not attached to them. You can be in the world, but you are not of the world. So you know who you are. You know you are That; it is you alone. When you realize that, it is the end of your practice. You cannot do anything more, and you need not.

At that point something happens to you. You experience a great truth. I cannot say what it is, and you cannot understand what it is until you reach that level by experiencing it. Then you will know that all nature and all humanity are a kind of mechanism. All the cells put together make this global body. If you just realize this, your spiritual quest ends. When you experience and realize that, the mind finds its perfect peace.

PART IV:

THE GREATEST JOY

27. The Butcher and the Yogi

Do you know the story of the butcher who initiated a great Yogi with a little ego? It's the story of Vyadan.

Once a *sadhu*, or spiritual seeker, who wanted very much to attain some ESP sat under a tree and began repeating a mantra. He had the dynamic will to sit there the entire day. Each day around noon he would get up and go to a nearby village to ask for food. *"Bavati biksham dehi,"* he called. "Mother, please give me a little food." And usually someone would bring him food. He would eat, then go back and sit again.

After months of this, one day a small test came. As he was meditating under a tree, something fell on the Yogi's shoulder. He examined it and saw that it was the excrement of a bird. He became annoyed and looked up. There was a crane sitting on a branch. Since he was observing silence, he said nothing. But he thought: "You little devil, how dare you do this!" And he looked with such anger that flames went from his eyes and completely burned the bird to ash. He saw the ash falling, and marveled: "Look at my *tapasya*, the strength from my austerities. How great I am; how fine are my supernatural powers." He was really convinced that he had achieved what there was to attain.

At noon he arose as usual, walked to the village, and stopped in front of a house. This time his tone was a little different. Normally a renunciate would say "A little food, please." But that day, he said simply, "Food, please."

Inside the housewife heard him and called: "Please wait, *sadhu*, I'll come soon."

"What, me wait?" he thought.

"I'm sorry I'm not the crane you can burn," came the answer from inside the house.

His temper dropped. "What did you say?"

"I'm sorry I'm not the bird."

He was almost fainting. He stood there quietly until she came out with the food. Then he said, "Mother, please, I don't want your food now. All the hunger is gone. But what did you mean about the bird?"

"Well, Swami. Don't you understand me yet? You can't get angry and burn me like you did the bird. Though I'm just an ordinary housewife, you can't burn me."

"You're not an ordinary housewife. How did you know what happened in the forest? I never told anybody."

"You don't need to. You reflect yourself clearly in my mind."

"Oh, what kind of *sadhana* do you practice? A new mantra to know the other person's mind?"

"I don't know any mantra at all, Swami. I'm just a housewife, as I told you. I always take care of my sick husband. He is bedridden. When you came I was attending him. I couldn't just drop that and come. That's why I asked you to wait. That's all. I'm just doing it as my duty. God placed me in this position and I'm fulfilling the responsibilities of a housewife. That's all I know. Probably I'm a Karma Yogi. I don't know. I'm just doing it, not for my sake."

"Is that all you do? I want to know more."

"Please, I'm not a scholar. I can't say anything more. If you want, go to the next town and see a butcher there by the name of Vyadan. Seek him and you'll get the answer."

"A butcher? You really want me to go to a butcher? One who cuts meat?"

"Yes, yes."

So he went and sought out Vyadan in the next town. The butcher was a hefty man, a fearful type, cutting meat, arguing over the price, fighting with people for every penny. ". . . Fifty cents for this. I can't sell it for less . . ."

"My goodness," wondered the Swami. "How is he going to teach me anything?" He had a little doubt. It was far to return home, but he was considering leaving when the butcher called to him, "Hey, *sadhu*, I'll be with you soon. The lady sent you to me. Don't worry. Stay. This is my job. I'll finish, then come to you. Please be seated."

The Swami was so stunned he had to sit or he probably would have fainted. So he sat quietly waiting. It took the butcher another hour to finish his business. The Yogi watched. Vyadan was a very staunch and stingy butcher—never giving way to anybody. He was strict with his price and with his weight. He was not an easy businessman to deal with. When everything was finished, he closed the shop, collected the money, put it in a bag, and then said, "Come on, we'll go home."

On their way, Vyadan bought some vegetables and they went into his house. "Please sit," he said. "I'll just cook these vegetables and feed my parents. They're too old. They're blind and can't see anything. I'll have to give them a bath and feed them. When I have finished, I'll come to you, so be seated."

He attended his parents, bathed them, fed them, and put them into bed. Then he came running. "Come on now, you too. Have a bath and something to eat, then we'll sit and talk."

"No, I'm not interested in having a bath or something to eat. My hunger is different. Bathe me with your wisdom. Feed me with your wisdom. I don't understand anything. I used to think that just by sitting under a tree and repeating a mantra I'd be doing *sadhana*. And I got *something*. But you people are doing all kinds of things. You are a butcher and she is a housewife. Yet you seem to know everything that I have in mind—and much, much more probably. How could you achieve this?"

Then Vyadan said, "I believe in God. God created everything and everybody—me and you. He, as the life force, functions through you and me and all things. We are all just gadgets. He is the main current. He gives us missions. He fixed this duty in the shop for me, and made me a butcher. So I'm doing this job. I say 'I,' but really He is doing it through me.

"And He has given me two old parents to care for. I'm satisfied with this. I do my butcher's work and take care of my parents. That's all I know. I don't even have time to repeat mantras. No, but I totally realize this is His will and that this is my duty according to God's plan. So my mind is totally clean. I'm not doing it for my sake. I'm doing it for the sake of the people. If I say,

'No, I can't do such work,' and close the shop, someone else will have to do it. He might not sell at the right price. For the sake of profit, he might buy animals treated with chemicals or painfully slaughtered.

"So I'm doing a fair business—it's my duty. It never taints my mind because I'm doing it as Karma Yoga, as service. That's why my mind is always calm and clean and peaceful. There are no disturbances in my mind. You scholarly people might say I'm a Yogi. If you want to label me, fine. But whoever comes in front of that clean mind, reflects themselves. And I see the image very well. You can't hide anything."

The aim of Yoga is always to keep the mind clean, calm, and peaceful.

28. Business Yoga

Work in your livelihood as Karma Yoga—selfless service. Do all work for the joy of doing it. Charge nothing for your labors; accept whatever you are paid. Choose work for someone or something that is worthwhile. Offer your work, your energy to Him, It, God, the All, everyone. Tell the one who pays you to pay whatever in conscience can be paid. If you need more than that to support yourself and your family, say so, and if necessary move on. Do your work step by step, with all patience. If you're fired, accept it. But do your best peacefully.

Maybe where you are working now does not have the best atmosphere. In time you can find more suitable work to fit your taste and temperament. But until then you can still work where you are and be a Yogi. Even if you sell steak or liquor, it doesn't mean you have to take it yourself. As a Karma Yogi, you serve there. Many people still love such things. Until you find better work, don't leave your present post, so if you don't find something right away, you won't be stranded. That's not Yogic either.

In a way working in such a place could give you more mental strength. Following your principles while living in such an atmosphere isn't easy. But if you can do it, you are a better Yogi. In one sense, if you don't believe in something, you should not contribute to it. But you cannot simply go without support. Because you refuse to do something, that doesn't mean the whole world will stop doing it. It's the attitude in your mind that is most important.

In some cases your conscience will make it very clear that you cannot stay, no matter what the economic situation. You should not sell your conscience for money. You may have to say, "I'm sorry, I don't want this job. Money is not really important to me. I can't do that." Yes, you may even lose your job. It doesn't matter, don't lose your principles. Many people have even given their lives to maintain their principles. Can't you lose a few dollars? Which is more important—the money you get from the business or your own personal mental and physical well-being? Don't think that money alone is going to bring everything. Many wealthy people are living in misery. However poor you are, your personal welfare is most important. Shun as poison anything that will interfere with your peace of mind. Everything has its own vibration.

If you resent your work or your employer, it is best not to stay. The work will not have charm or beauty. You can't love the work if you can't love the person who gives you the work. If you feel resentment, analyze the cause. If you have a proper reason and can't get over it, don't continue there. Your attitude will just waste both your time and your employer's, because no matter how beautiful such work is your vibration is carried with your work. If you type a letter with resentment, the letter itself will carry that resentment. Try to change your attitude, but if you really have good cause for resentment, then change your job. Try to have a good and respectful relationship with your employer. Don't always think the capitalists are out to exploit you. Without capitalists you would not even be working. The employer is there to give employment. It is his money and energy that started the place of work which now provides jobs. You give energy, but for that energy he gives you food. Try to have some compassion and understanding. If he makes a mistake, help him realize this by passive means, if you can, but never through hatred. That's Yoga in business.

You are the master of your destiny. You are the cause of your own poverty, wealth, or fame. Open a new chapter in your life. Choose your environment. Choose your occupation. Your temperament will guide you. As your life changes and as you grow you may find your tastes and temperament changing. You may have been doing something different two or three years before, but now your inclinations are different. Let yourself do whatever comes naturally from within.

You don't need to copy someone else. If it's your temperament, it will come automatically. Everyone has something special. Each person is unique. Nobody can occupy your position. Don't put yourself down. If you believe in the Cosmic Will, you will discover that unseen hand operating through you. See what it is, and let it happen through you.

Sometimes when we first offer ourselves to God we seem to run into problems. We may encounter suffering and losses. It's easy to be devoted when we are always gaining from God. If our businesses thrive, it's very easy to love Him. But if we go to church and offer ourselves totally to God, and the next day lose $10,000 in business, we ask, "What kind of God is this?" The proof of our devotion is that we still love Him regardless of what happens. He may test us in the beginning.

If you are really trying to apply these principles to your life, people will respect you. Employers say they want to hire more Yogis. If you show that you are a Yogi on your résumé, they will value you. Take a useful job just to serve.

Why do you need food, clothing, and shelter? You want to live to serve others. You have to eat to live. You need clothes, a car, a garage for the car. How can you do that without the money? You prepare yourself and equip yourself with enough energy to give energy back. Your eating, sleeping, drinking, and breathing are not selfish actions if you do them with the intention: "I am only keeping myself fit to serve others. If I am not going to serve others, I don't need to eat. I don't need to sleep. I don't need to have a house. I don't even need to live."

If you are serving totally with dedication and still not earning enough to survive, certainly you can say, "I am becoming weak. I won't be able to serve you longer, sir. Who is the loser, me or you?" If he still won't change, what can you do? Stop serving. Don't force your service anywhere. But usually such selfless service melts even the hardest heart. Everyone has a soft corner somewhere. You find that soft place through your sincerity and love. Even the most deadly, dangerous, and hateful person can be absorbed by love. Ultimately Truth will win; it's nature's way.

So do your work with all patience. Do it in a meditative way.

If you have a mantra, repeat it mentally while you are doing your work. Love and salute your tools. Nothing is inert; everthing has a kind of feeling. When you deal with things, feel as if you're touching God. Feel that the work you are doing is the worship of God, that you are doing the work for His sake, and that He is receiving the benefit of your work. Your work will become Karma Yoga.

Whatever your function in a business, help that business grow. Whether you are a secretary or the manager, think of the welfare of the business. Consider how it can grow better and best perform its duty. Be scrupulously honest. Instead of using the office facilities for your own personal reasons, put the business first. If all day Friday your use the office telephone for your weekend appointments, you are not a good businessman. You are bringing loss and in a way even stealing from the business. Always think of the benefit the others should get.

When you are a Karma Yogi, you may find yourself chosen for more responsible posts. You might take in a profit, which is all right in Yoga. But profit should not be your motive. Your motive should be for the benefit of the community. The seller should put himself in the position of the buyer. The buyer should put himself in the position of the seller. Always recognize the needs of the other person. Even if you are able to do so, don't exploit. That's Yogic business. Certainly you should have some profit, but not 100, 200 or 300 per cent. The confidence and good will of the customer is worth more than the money—it is a great profit.

29. *The Art of Giving*

Many of our international peace talks fail. Why? The people who talk of peace do not seem to have peace themselves. Each wants to grab something from the other. They go to their meetings with anxiety, thinking: "What can I gain from this person?" Sometimes they can't even agree on the shape of the table at which they will meet. Even children are better. To achieve peace, people must go with the idea of giving—not grabbing.

Through giving we have joy. I have seen that in my Master's life. Instead of Sivananda, we often called him *Givananda*. He always enjoyed giving because there's such joy in giving and loving. By giving we never make enemies. Nations should learn this. We should always give whatever we have; we don't need to grab from each other. Through caring and sharing we find ease within ourselves, and among our fellow beings.

Begin with yourself. If you have a surplus, choose the right people and give it to them: "See, I have no use for this. Come on, please use it." That way we share our energy; we share everything we have with others. If we do this, there won't be any haves and have-nots—there will only be the haves. It's a form of communism, no doubt—but without any violence. Communism believes in forcing people to redistribute what there is. That's not real sharing. Giving should come from the heart. You should give willingly. Then there won't be any animosity.

And the people who receive will also be grateful. If the government forces us to give our property, then passes it on, the recipients won't be grateful to us because force was used. On the other hand, if we share willingly with others, there is certainly enough for everyone on this planet. We should feel the whole world is ours. Wherever you feel it is necessary to help, go there and work. This practice is needed today. After all, which is more important—to feed your own brother or to walk on the moon? Sometimes the heart aches to see such ignorance.

If you ever think of donating something, before the left hand knows, give with the right hand. The gift should be given with the whole heart. Don't even call it helping. Call it service because you are the one who benefits by it. If a man begs from you, and you give him something, don't think you are helping him. He is helping you. Hasn't he given you an opportunity to show your generosity? If no one is there to receive, how could you donate? The giver should thank the receiver.

But don't give by knocking on the door and pushing yourself in. Human beings are not inanimate or just animals. They are endowed with a little extra knowledge and discrimination. You have full liberty to use your discrimination for the sake of the person who is receiving from you. If a drunk man comes and asks you for another ten dollars, you will certainly know that he plans to take it and go directly back to the bar. If you think that is not healthy for him, you should refuse. Even in your refusal you are thinking of his benefit more than your own.

Charity should be given with proper discrimination and it should be timely. In India we say, what's the use of having drinking water stations during the rainy season? There's plenty of water everywhere. Put your drinking water stations in the desert. The needy should get what you are giving at the right time. What's the use of bringing me a nice warm woolen blanket when the temperature is 110°? I could buy the entire set of holy scriptures and give them to a one-year-old baby on her birthday. What's the use? I'm giving scriptures, it's true, but she can't use them now.

So always discriminate. Think before you give. Know the person well and find out how he or she is going to use your gift. Blind love can spoil a person. If you want to spoil a baby, give the baby whatever it wants to eat. The baby will want chocolate candy more and more and more. If you keep on giving, the next day you will be taking the baby to the doctor. Understand the gift of charity in this light.

If you ever have selfish expectations when you give something, that will surely disturb your peace later on. Anytime you expect something in return for your efforts it's *karma*. This is why we come across so many labor unions, labor departments, and arbitration boards. Whenever people expect something, there will always be some kind of tussle when they don't get exactly what they expect. He expects more of your work; you expect more of his money. So there is a continual tugging between the employer and the employee. And to undo the tangles that come from this, you have to go to court. You've heard of many labor cases in court, but never of a case fighting over free service.

Nobody goes to court in the name of service. Service is just one-sided. You just give for the sake of giving; no expectation whatsoever. There is never any trouble, either for you or for the one who is receiving. If you are doing your work as service, the one who receives never feels obliged. That's the best possible service. Whenever you give something, don't make the other one feel obligated in any way. Don't even look at his face waiting for a nice thank you, a smile, or a little appreciation. Why? If you miss that smile or nodding of the head or the thank you, you won't be happy because you expected it. Suppose you give something to someone who is busy. He may just take it quickly, and continue what he is doing while you are waiting for some acknowledgment of your service. Then you are disappointed because you didn't get something in return.

Making the receiver obliged to you is *karma*, and not Karma Yoga or true service. Karma Yoga is just doing for the sake of doing, for the joy of serving. That's the very highest reward you can get. Suppose you offer a gift, and the person says, "Hey, is this all you can bring?" Still you feel fine, you're not bothered by it. You already have the joy of giving something. Don't be bothered by what he says. You wanted to give; you gave. You're happy. Can anybody stop your happiness? Only you can stop and disturb that joy—by expecting something in return. The minute you expect something in return you lose the joy, you lose your peace of mind. Before giving you build up some tension. As you wrap the present you think, "Oh, how beautiful it is. He is going to really love this." Even before you wrap the present, when you were out shopping for the gift, you assumed things and built some tension. With such complications, the mind is not at ease even in what it is doing for another. You are nervous, until you put it in his hand, and he looks at you and says, "Oh, it is beautiful, thank you so much." Finally you are relieved. "Ah, I really got him something good." Until that moment there was tension and anxiety. "Will he appreciate it? Will it make him happy?" Even afterward, "Did he really like it?"

All these anxieties are due to your expectations. Until he appreciated the present you felt anxiety. Only when he smiled gratefully did you feel some happiness for a little while. But that is borrowed happiness—from outside yourself. It won't last long, and you'll want a little more the next day. So you will have to buy a bigger present. You will want more and more and more. Even if you achieve his good will, appreciation, or love, you'll fear losing it. You won't want anyone else to look at him, or give him a present. "What if she gives him a bigger present?" Jealousy enters, the fear of losing him. So when do you feel happy? Neither before nor after. It's all a kind of business.

Watch out for business gifts. The gift is not just for the sake of giving. You go with a nice parcel today and come with a small petition tomorrow. Even God is not spared from such business gifts. You light a beautiful little candle for God, and soon after, even while He is appreciating your candle, you say, "Don't keep looking at that, listen to my request. I don't have time to wait to ask this. I have to run the office. You can look at the candle later. Listen to me, this is what I want . . ."

It is like that everywhere. In Sri Lanka there is a well-known temple. The front entrance is always covered with seven screens. The esoteric meaning behind this is that seven sheaths hide the inner Self. Each year there is a competition among devotees to see who will donate the screens. It's a particularly terrible competition to see who will donate the front screen because everything else is hidden behind that foremost screen, on which there is a big beautiful painting of the form of Lord Subramanya.

The competition is not simply for the painting, but to show who gave it because the donor's name is printed there clearly for all to see. Donated by Mr. So-and-so, 98 Main Street, Such-and-

Such a Store, Colombo—5. His full address, his business, and maybe even his telephone number is written there.

One year, a person who donated the front screen came and spoke to me.

"Swamiji, did you go to Katarangama this year?"

"Yes, I was there for the Lord's festival."

"Did you see the screen in front?"

"Yes, it's so beautiful."

"That's me."

"Oh, you are the one whose name is on the screen?"

"Yes, don't you think it is truly beautiful?"

"Yes, the picture is beautiful. But more than that is there. I saw your name and address. What a great sin you have committed."

"What are you saying? Why do you tell me this?"

"It's a terrible sin. Sin doesn't mean that you did something to destroy somebody or anything like that. But you are ruining yourself. You are going to become a very big debtor."

"I don't understand you, Swamiji. Please tell me."

"Okay, take a pencil and paper. We'll get into some mathematical calculations. Do you sometimes advertise your store in the paper?"

"Yes."

"How much do you pay for a column of one inch?"

"A one-inch column in the *Daily News* is very expensive, Swamiji. They charge a thousand dollars."

"Ah. Take for example something like *Life* magazine. How much for one full page ad?"

"Maybe fifty thousand dollars."

"For that one page which will be seen for maybe a week, fifty thousand dollars. Now how many people are seeing your screen? Say about ten million. And the screen you have put there has your name on it. Do you know how many millions of people are going to see that throughout the year? Is it not a big advertisement for you? God is not sending you a bill immediately. But He will keep an account of how many people have seen that how many times. The advertisement cost for your firm will be debited in your account there. You might have donated a hundred dollars for the screen, which will be credited to your account, no doubt, but the indebtedness of your account grows daily. If there are ten thousand people each day who pass the screen and read your name, figure at least a dollar per head; ten thousand dollars debit in your account each day; in a few days, fifty thousand dollars debit. For the whole year I don't know how many millions you are going to have to pay back. How are you going to pay for all of this? When are you going to pay? You will have to be born again and again. Do you think this is a profitable business?"

"Swamiji, I understand your point. What am I going to do? I can't just go and take the screen away now."

"We think that God has no sense of calculation. He's a first-class businessman. Remember, what you give, you get. If you give ten per cent, you get only ten per cent of God. If you give twenty-five per cent, you get twenty-five per cent of God. He's a fair businessman. Equal proportions, one per cent for one per cent. Suppose you give a hundred per cent, what will you get? One hundred per cent of God.

"And your hundred per cent is worth nothing—maybe about one hundred fifty pounds of flesh and bones, and some rotten stuff here and there that even the garbage people don't want to take. Yet with all this rubbish, it doesn't matter. He accepts your percentage.

'Are you the one who gave to Me completely?'

'Yes, I'm totally surrendering to You, Sir.'"

He accepts your surrendering. You are not of much use to God, but remember He is a fair businessman. "He has given his hundred per cent to Me. What am I to do? I have to give My hundred per cent to him, otherwise I'm unfair." So He gives Himself to you, 100 per cent. This is the secret of the devotion business.

30. The Art of Receiving

One of the main purposes of Yoga is to keep the mind calm. There are certain gifts that, if accepted, make you feel obligated. If you are unable to fulfill that obligation, you are disturbed. According to the Yoga precepts of Patanjali, that is the reason you are advised not to accept gifts; if you do, unconsciously you become obliged to the giver. Later you have to go out of your way to do something to satisfy that person.

As you know, such gifts are business gifts. The people are not giving just for the joy of giving. The giver expects something in return. If a young man sends a nice bouquet of flowers to a young woman, it's not always simply because he feels joyful in sending it. He wants to win her affection. If he's not successful, he feels disturbed: "How dare you accept all my gifts and don't even send me a letter." For whose sake is such a gift? And if she accepts his gifts, she may feel obliged to him. If you ever receive a gift that has some strings attached, return it and your mind won't be disturbed.

Certain types of gifts will not disturb your mind. Those you can accept. Someone is just expressing his love or reverence for you and expects nothing back. He feels he should do it, and it is an opportunity for him perhaps to fulfill an obligation he feels to you. Accept it. But if somehow you personally feel obliged receiving it, you are receiving more for yourself than for the sake of the one who gave it. To maintain your own peace of mind, you should return the gift. You may not have the opportunity to give him something back, and you will feel guilty.

Sometime you may be really hungry and someone wants to give you some food. You can accept that, too. Of course you should feel grateful, but even then don't feel obliged and lose your peace. Sometimes people give money to worthy organizations that convert their money into meritorious actions. If you are receiving the donation for the organization, you can accept it without feeling any obligation because it's for the general cause. The donor should feel grateful because his money is being converted into meritorious acts; that merit goes to the giver. Whether he knows it or not, there is a divine accountant who takes count of everything.

You may not be sure how a gift will affect your mind. Whenever you receive something from anyone always try to give something back. If possible, give even more than you get. That's Yoga. For example, if you have borrowed something, when you return it, it should be more beautiful than when you borrowed it. When you borrow a book, for example, the first thing you should do is see that the book is bound properly. If there's a torn page, repair it, put a jacket on it. Only then start reading.

If we receive and don't give something back, we become debtors. Certain things are priceless and we can never pay them back fully. How can we repay all we get from God? When we take a small candle or a scented stick, some fruit, or a small offering to the church or synagogue does it mean we are paying back all we got? No, we just return what we can, so that we will not be debtors. That frees us from the feeling "I got, but what can I do in return?" It's not a fee. If it were, we wouldn't get anything unless we paid the fee. An offering is simply giving according to our capacity, and it will keep the mind peaceful and free from feeling indebted.

In the Hindu scripture we are told, don't go empty-handed to a baby, a king, a saintly person, or to God. Bring an offering, no matter how simple or rich, but whatever it is, it should come from the sweat of your toil. When you go to see a baby, take something—not because the baby is consciously giving you something, but because you will be happy in the baby's presence. You will be inspired. You are in the divine presence. A baby is like the sun dispelling the clouds. Being near a baby makes you feel like a baby—you forget all your problems.

Don't go empty-handed to see a king because at least you are earning some sort of recognition by meeting him. And he won't send you away empty-handed. He will give you a favor of some kind. For example, every time I visited the Pope, he always gave me some token. Naturally I knew he would do so, so how could I go empty-handed? Always take something in return.

If you visit a saintly or holy person you will surely get some vibration and good ideas to elevate your life, something that you can't get anywhere else—not at your colleges or at Macy's or Gimbels. No, you are getting something unique. Return anything you can. It can be just a flower.

And always bring something to God. When you go before God's presence, perhaps in a church, temple, synagogue, or mosque, don't go empty-handed. Your donation may be used for any purpose. That's none of your business. The priest may collect the money and go to the movies. If he is doing something wrong and misusing what is given in the name of God, that is his business. He will have to face God for that. Why should you worry? You have finished your obligation.

During the last century hundreds of people would come everyday and evening to Sri Ramakrishna's ashram. As they arrived, naturally they would bring all kinds of offerings—fruits, flowers, money, food, whatever—because they didn't want to come without bringing something. Among them was a very poor man who had been coming almost every day to sit and listen. He enjoyed Ramakrishna's company and wisdom. Ramakrishna noticed him and called him over, "Are you a working man?"

"I pull the rickshaw and get one or two rupees each day; barely enough to support my family. I work but I'm very poor."

"Hmmm. That's all right, but can you spare a penny?" asked the sage.

"Well—I can."

"Probably a penny is too much for you. Tomorrow you buy some areca nuts." In India the areca nut is broken into small pieces, almost a powder, and people usually chew it with betel leaves and a little lime. It makes the mouth reddish in color and has some medicinal effect. Ramakrishna thought the man might be accustomed to chewing these nuts. He asked the man to spend a penny. He could get at least ten nuts for a penny, and break each nut into ten pieces. "Every day you come, bring one piece to me," he told the man.

"What are you going to do with that? One hundredth of a penny. You already have plenty."

"Yes, I have plenty. It's not that I don't have—it's for you. You should not come empty-handed. If whenever you come, you arrive without something, you become my debtor. One day you will have to pay it back to me. Maybe you will have to take another birth as my servant. *Karma* is *karma;* an action has its reaction."

That's the reason we say when you receive, always offer something; don't go as a debtor. But it depends on your capacity. If you are a millionaire, you will be able to give more than the poor man. But whoever you are, give something. Then you will be free from obligation and your mind will be clear.

The more you give, the more you get; that's nature's law. If you are a good channel you won't keep anything for yourself except what you need—you will pass along the rest. Then more things will come to you. It's like a fountain that you have drawn forth. The more you draw, the more it comes. You never feel the want. Sometimes you will get so much, you will be tired of giving. You will have to say, "God, what is this? You are pushing me so much. I don't know where to give. There are no people to receive." But at no point try to stop it from flowing through you. If you stop the flow, you'll notice that it gets stagnant and stinks. Things love to move freely.

So all the things keep coming to you thinking you are a wonderful person because you won't hold them or cling to them. They will just want to come and sit under your shade for a little while, like the birds coming to rest on a branch. And the branch allows them to fly wherever they want.

But if you try to imprison anything, they will hesitate to come, and whatever you have imprisoned will try to run away from you. Imagine a man who thinks himself very rich and keeps bundles of currency in his safe. Each day he opens the safe, counts the money, and closes it. Even at night he gets up to see whether the money is there or not, and locks the safe again. He may enjoy seeing the bills in the safe. But ask the currency notes, "Are you happy inside the safe?" They may say, "I don't know why he keeps us here. We came to this miserly, stingy, greedy man. He never lets us go out and move about freely. He has locked us in this iron prison. We don't know what to do. God, won't You save us? Is this our *karma* to be caught in his hands?"

Then one midnight slowly the safe door opens. The currency will say, "Ahh, thank you. Did God send you? Quickly, take us away before that fellow sees you." Yes, it's not entirely a joke. Everything that you put under lock and key grumbles at you. They all want freedom as you do. They want free movement—not to be bound by anything.

So when things come to you, just let them come. When they are in your possession, take good care of them while you are using them; don't just leave them lying about. But when you are finished, leave them free to move again. Use things as long as you want. Allow them to stay as long as they want to stay with you. But the minute they say, "I'm a little tired of being here, let me go to another place," say, "Sure, go. Your freedom is there."

When you do that, you know what happens? They may leave you because you don't imprison them. They might somehow become fascinated with another house. But there they are locked up, and one day they escape and go to yet another house, and are again locked up. Then they realize, "My goodness, I should have stayed with that fellow who really gave me freedom." So they come back to you. When you don't cling to anything, everything comes back and wants to remain with you—even if you say, "Why don't you go?"

"No, wherever I go, I get caught. I'll just stay with you."

"That's contentment. If you don't imprison things and don't run after things, they will love to be with you. I'm just interpreting the scriptural sayings in a little different way. The *Sannyas Upanishad*, speaking of the glory of renunciation, says, "If a man is totally dispassionate and not clinging onto anything—which is complete renunciation—he will find the Goddess of Learning and the Goddess of Wealth sitting at his feet waiting to serve him."

31. Living in the Present

All that you do begins within you in the form of a seed. *Karma,* or the reaction of your actions, forms seeds that are stored in the granary of your mind—the *karmic* bag. You have to deliver one seed after another. Sometimes you deliver them in groups— group *karma*—sometimes one by one. The delivery time depends upon the strength of the seed. A more mature seed germinates quickly, so if you do ten *karmas* or actions today, maybe the eighth and sixth will bear fruit tomorrow. The first and second may not bear fruit for ten years. You don't always get a reaction in the same order that you perform the actions; it depends on the intensity with which the action is performed and what kind of *karma* it is. If you eat some undesirable food and soon thereafter put your finger into a candle flame, your first *karma* is eating the food and your second is putting your finger in the flame. But the second *karma* brings a result immediately. The first *karma* may not germinate for two or three days; then you'll get a stomach-ache. But whatever you have done, you will surely have to accept its reaction—the reward or the insult— sometime.

No teacher, no guru, no scripture, no temple, no synagogue, no church can purge you of your *karma.* Even God will not take away your *karma.* Only by sowing seeds of selfless actions today can you purge it.

Knowing about *karma* can be helpful. If by chance you are insulted or struck by someone for what seems to be no apparent reason, you can reason, "Probably it's my *karma.* I must have hurt somebody earlier and escaped from being hurt in return. Now it comes back to me and I accept it." There is no effect without a cause—no one will hurt you if you are really innocent. You may be innocent today, but days before, years before, even the life before, you probably weren't innocent. So you can say to your oppressor, "Okay, you helped me purge my *karma*. Thank you so much." You sow better *karma* when you don't return hatred with hatred. A fight won't stop a fight. Accepting injury without returning it is highest spiritual practice. It takes strength to do that. Pouring love on hate is like pouring water on fire.

Ultimately you discover how to perform perfect actions, without sowing any *karma*. An act becomes perfect when you do it entirely with joy and without any expection. All other acts—however wonderful they are, however beautiful they look, however they are labelled—are still imperfect because they affect your mind. You may wonder, "What about good acts?" That's like a parrot who says, "Take this dirty, steel cage and give me a golden cage." It looks pretty, but it's still a cage. Anything done with expectation will bind you. The cause of birth and death is your *karma*—actions done expecting something in return.

Of course it's not easy to renounce both the bad and good right away. So, in the beginning at least we are advised to overcome bad actions by doing things for the sake of merit and virtue. However, to be truly free, we must act without any expectation, renouncing both the bad and the good fruits of our actions. That's Karma Yoga. We do everything for the sake of God or the sake of humanity. We expect nothing in return. And whatever we do is done perfectly as a service to God because we have no anxieties about future results.

Most people act in their own best interests. The very idea of future benefits is exciting; people tend to build castles in their minds. But, as the Muslim story of Alnasur shows, even the mere thought of future benefits can make you lose everything.

Once a man named Alnasur went to the market where he was given the opportunity to do an ordinary laborer's job by picking up some things, carrying them to another place, and putting them down. He was given five dollars. That was the most he had ever had in his hand at one time. "My goodness, what shall I do?" he thought. "Let me buy some eggs from this market with these five dollars, take them home to my village, and sell them. So he bought the eggs, arranged them in a well-padded basket, put the basket on his head, and began walking home.

After a while he became a little tired, and he sat down to rest with the package nearby. Even on his way, he had been dreaming, "When I get back, I'll sell these in my little village where they don't have such fine eggs. I can easily sell these for double the price, and make ten dollars—a 100 per cent profit." He was so excited by this prospect that he got up and walked until he tired again. Again he put the basket down in front of him and leaned back to rest, continuing to dream, "With the ten dollars I'll return to the market and get ten dollars worth of eggs, return to the village, sell them, and get twenty dollars. But with that twenty dollars, I won't buy eggs. That's menial business. I'll buy something more desired in the own, return, and sell it—maybe for triple this time, because with eggs I can only make 100 per cent. If I buy some cosmetics, I can easily make 300–400 per cent."

He sat there leaning against a tree with the basket near and continued to dream. In his dream he very soon made several thousand dollars. He became a rich man, and he said, "Now that I'm really very rich, I can't just live alone. Naturally I should look for a beautiful girl to marry. And no doubt when they all see how wealthy I am, Mirastar, the richest man in town, will come and offer his lovely daughter to me. After a little hesitation on my part, I will marry her. Then, of course, she'll give me a nice baby. When I come from my office she will bring the baby to me to play with. Sometimes I might come home a little tired, and if she brings the baby, I'll just say, 'Oh, I'm too tired. I don't want the baby now. Take him away.' If she says, 'No, please be with him now' and insists, I will insist too. 'No, no, no. I am too tired.' If she continues to insist, I will just kick her out—like *this*." And Alnasur kicked so hard that his foot went into the basket of eggs and broke them.

That's the story of Alnasur. By seeking benefits in the future, we can't live well in present. I'm not saying building castles in the sky is never good at all. If you build constructive castles with good ideas—just one step at a time—it can be useful to you. A little expectation is good for your motivation. But don't insist on some personal benefit or you will be easily disappointed and frustrated. As the beautiful hymn says: Just one step is enough for me. Let me not go all the way. Just show me the next couple steps, and when I go there I'll be ready to see further.

The joy of doing a job well is the best reward. Nobody can take that satisfaction away from you. If you wait to be satisfied by results, you are certainly going to be dissatisfied. That's why in many situations, no matter how small or large, people become disturbed and unhappy as they move toward their objective. If you are ever disturbed by such emotion—or by the excitement of anticipation—know that you are not being a Karma Yogi at that moment.

The Karma Yogi acts without attachment to the fruits of his labors. He performs actions just for the joy of performing them—not for later benefits. His mind is in the present, and his actions are perfect. His service is for God or all of humanity. So the Karma Yogi must pay even more attention to detail than the most miserly businessman does to his business. He must do a job ten times better than the person who is sowing seeds of *karma*.

People who act with their minds on the future benefits don't even think about what they're doing. They thus lose efficiency. Go slow, be steady. If you think fast, you lose all your power. Don't even think about the fruits. If some fruit comes to you, you may certainly taste it, but don't reach for it. Do one thing at a time. Concentrate your efforts.

32. *The Greatest Joy*

You quickly learn your weaknesses while serving others. The world is like a big mirror—it shows you your ugly spots, your weaknesses. Through service you can learn to recognize your own weaknesses and work to correct them.

Sometimes the best test is what you call menial work. You often hear how great sages tested themselves in this way. To see if he had become proud after becoming a big guru, Ramakrishna went to slum areas and washed the toilets with his hair. Jesus washed the feet of his followers. Great men have done this. So go, take the dirtiest, nastiest job. Remember that you are not doing the job for the sake of the work as much as for yourself. It's easy to simply go to a corner and meditate. But there's another form of meditation—action. During Karma Yoga you meditate on what you're doing. You watch your feelings and watch your mind. It's a mental training program.

Practice Karma Yoga whenever you have the opportunity. In this practice you see your limitations and drawbacks, you test yourself in the field. You will understand your attitudes and moods better than when you're alone. Through Karma Yoga your heart, mind, and body will soon be cleaned. Of course, you should not totally ignore other practices, and you need not do Karma Yoga twenty-four hours each day. If you are very tired or have some sort of emotional or psychological problem, come back, sit down quietly, and analyze your problem.

"I went there to serve him, but for some reason I became annoyed—probably when he didn't thank me. Yes, I was expecting his thanks. That's not right. That's how my mind became disturbed. Next time, I'll do the same thing, but I won't look for thanks." This way you shape your mind well. By such analysis you can soon reduce the tendency that disturbs your peace. If you ignore the disburbances and simply try to continue your service, the problem will come back again and again.

Making a mistake is not really bad. The minute you realize you have made a mistake, think, "Why? How? What caused this mistake? Where did I err? If I hadn't done that, this would not have happened. Okay, next time I won't allow that to happen." An intelligent person will learn something from a mistake, but a fool will make the same mistake again and again. We fall down and we get up and walk. Let our failures be stepping stones to our success. All the great people, the sages and saints, have also fallen many times before they achieved their goals.

Often you are still selfish in a subtle way even though you think you are not attached to the fruits. If you insist others should be happy because of what you're doing, then you are still attached. You will build up anxiety which makes you unfit to help. Instead, it's better just to think, "Well, I have done my duty to my satisfaction; I am not the destiny maker." If a man has done certain things and is destined to be unhappy for some time, you cannot make him happy however much you try. The satisfaction of having tried within your limit should be enough for you. Do what you can within your limit, then transfer the case to the Higher Court.

Use wisdom to analyze your motives. Don't always think simply which yogurt tastes better to eat. That's not deep analysis. Find out what will bring peace and joy to yourself and others. Always analyze in those terms. Karma Yoga alone is enough to save your soul. You won't have to force yourself to serve others if you know the benefits of such service. You'll be frightened to be selfish for fear of losing your peace. The greatest joy in life is doing something for somebody else. Unfortunately, many people have never tasted real joy, but once you do, you will never want to do something only for yourself again. You will look for opportunities to serve. Whether it's day or night you won't want to miss that supreme joy of dedicated service. It will haunt your personality forever. Become a public food. Offer yourself to others. Your life can be a beautiful fruit for all humanity to enjoy. Even your eating can be an offering. Who is digesting your food? "I am the digestive fire," says the Lord. "I am also in the stomach." Don't think that you are eating for your own sake. The food goes into this divine fire.

Even when you take a shower, think, "I am washing the Lord's temple. I am dressing the Lord's temple. He is seated here. I am feeding Him." When you go to sleep, think, "I am putting Him to sleep." Thus, every act becomes an offering; your very life becomes an offering.

That's the trick of Karma Yoga. When you do everything for the sake and joy of just doing it—as benefit for the whole world and not for your own personal benefit—you retain your joy. Don't think that you *get* joy by doing this. The joy is in you always. You must do something because you can't simply sit there quietly doing nothing. Your actions allow you to retain the Supreme Joy.

To taste that joy, begin by setting apart a week once every month or two. Say, "This is my Karma Yoga week. I should be totally selfless the entire week. I won't do anything for my sake." Or just choose one day—like a fasting day—and say, "This is my selfless day." Everybody should set aside some time for this, just to get a taste of that joy. Then you can expand it more and more.

When you do this, don't worry about others, such as your friends or even your family members. Someone in your family might say, "Hey, you're constantly doing for others. Don't you know that you have a husband, you have a wife, you have children. They are missing their benefits." It's not that you should ignore them. But don't continually spend all your money, energy, and time serving one or two people alone. The husband might demand all the wife's service. "You are my wife. You take care of me first." You can simply say, "Sir, there are certain things that you deserve and need. I do them for you. But the rest of the time other people need me more. Sometimes, my dear, you demand too much." You can say that. There's nothing wrong in it. No one can own you. If there is an opportunity to do something more important for the public, that's God's work. Don't forget you have first responsibilities to your husband or wife, but see that they don't demand more than they are due. Your life must be well divided this way. It's something like having five children. If one child constantly demands your attention—"Carry me, Mom. Carry me."—and you always do as he asks, you will ignore all the other children.

Subramanya Barati, a great and saintly poet, lived in India earlier in this century. He had foresight and his words were awakening. He knew a great deal about Yoga. In one poem he wrote, "The essence of scriptures is Karma Yoga. That alone can save us Service, service, service, that is enough for us."

Master Sivananda always said, "Serve and love. Service comes first. Serve with love, because without love you cannot serve. Without control of your passions and selfishness you cannot serve. You become a Yogi just by serving. Everything else comes automatically. Lose not even a single opportunity to serve others."

33. *Marriage on the Path*

Some people marry to have a partner in a dedicated life, a companion in a life of service. Marriages motivated only by physical beauty, money, or other worldly reasons will be bondage. But if there's a spiritual attraction, the marriage will be made in heaven. A wedding is between two reflections of God. Two pairs of eyes see one vision. They are dedicated to serve one another and the humanity at large.

Such a marriage is a supreme way—two co-operating partners and one goal. Two minds come together to help each other realize their true nature. Going side by side with the right partner is a good way to reach God quickly. When the husband's and the wife's love for each other blends together and becomes love of God, marriage is a divine institution.

Choose someone with your heart. If you always use your head to decide everything, you will always find differences, because egoism resides in the head. That's why you never hear of "sweet heads." But when people come together in the heart, they are real sweethearts. A totally headless heart is too emotional, but let the heart be there first. Then in God's name come together and enjoy that relationship.

There is mating everywhere in the universe—it's natural. Electrons make love by twirling around neutrons. God is that love drawing you together and urging you to give of yourself. The minute you are married you are not only yourself anymore. You lose your smaller self. You may even give up your old name and take another. But the more you give, the more you get.

Don't let competition enter your marriage and divide you. The women's and men's liberation movements are missing the point. It's not Yoga. In a way wanting others to approve of you, or blaming someone else for your problems is a form of self-condemnation. After all, what is the difference between man and woman? At most a few pounds and some physical features. Beyond that they are of the same mind, intelligence, and soul. In Yoga the aim is to purify the mind in order to reveal the spirit, which is neither male nor female. At the spiritual level, you rise above the body and mind. There can be no inequality.

One and the same essence appears as man and as woman. They come together to help each other. This is the play of the essence. One and the same seem to separate, and then come together. It's a game. We should remember we are all the same, and only playing in different roles. Actually, in spirit we are all wedded together. We can have hundreds of husbands and hundreds of wives. When we feel we are spirit, then the whole world is ours. That's the real marriage.

Being devoted to God doesn't mean ignoring your partner. See God in your mate, you'll both be happy. If you can't see God there, at least see a God-sent companion for you. Respect your partner. Win the other's love and affection. Even if the other doesn't believe in God or appreciate your Yoga practices, just do your part and show your love. Fulfill your responsibilities and give the other plenty of freedom. By forcing anything on someone you just earn displeasure and resistance. Be a good companion. By your good example your partner will probably learn to love God too.

Certainly there will be some differences in your marriage; otherwise everything would be boring. But you don't have to prolong them. Remember that no quarrel is ever one-sided. There is always some wrong on both sides; it's only a matter of per cent. Even if your fault amounts to only 20 per cent, don't wait for the other to correct the 80 per cent. If you think, "Why doesn't he change first?" then you are not being a Yogi. If you want to be peaceful, admit your fault. Go and say, "I'm sorry. Maybe I provoked you by my mistake."

It's like two palms striking against each other. There's no noise without both of them coming together. One might move slowly and the other quickly. One hand might say, "I was just standing there. I never even took a step. The other came and struck me." But why can't *you* move back? It's simple. You don't have to be stubborn.

When there are two egos projecting, there is going to be a clash. At least one of them should calm down and admit its fault —however small. Maybe at that moment, the other won't be able to accept it. So just leave. Calmly walk away from the situation. The other one will sit and think, "What is this? Everytime I get violent, she seems to be very calm and peaceful. I can't go on like this." Everyone has that beautiful heart inside. "Honey, I'm sorry," he will say. "I was a little upset at the office." It happens often. You get upset where there is no outlet for your anger so you come home and break loose. As a couple, one should be the outlet for the other's egoism, anger, or outburst. In that way you can help each other. But it takes a lot of courage. If you don't yet have that courage and strength to keep your peace, then temporarily go out, get yourself settled, and meet afterward.

I've seen many cases in which one partner through keeping a beautiful attitude has won the other. Since everyone has a soft corner, you can always touch it if you have the patience. You don't always have to part if there is difficulty at home. People get angry when one is grabbing from the other, thinking, "I want my thing." When that selfishness comes, even the most beautiful loving couple cannot be loving any longer. Don't wait for the other to give before you give. Go first; at least you'll find peace. Then at least 50 per cent of the family has found peace.

If your companion says he hates you, ask: "Why do you want to hate me? Does it make you happy? Okay, if you can be happy hating me, then do so, because I love you." It really takes courage to do that. Hatred will not eliminate hatred. You can never make someone love you by hating him. Don't retaliate. Just let your nature be giving and loving. That's God's love, an outpouring with no expectation for anything back. Love knows no bargain—it only gives and gives and gives. That's what is called universal love.

Once a man went to wash at the river and it was flooding. As he bent down he saw a scorpion being carried away by the flood, and he felt pity. He put out his hand and scooped the scorpion out of the water. But as he did so, it stung him. By reflex he shook his hand and the scorpion fell back into the water. Again he felt pity. "I'm sorry. No, you can't die." He took it out again. Another sting. The hand shook. Again the scorpion fell into the water. He bent down to take it one more time. His friend, who was standing behind him watching everything, said, "You fool. Every time you pick it up, it stings you. Don't you have any common sense?"

"I don't know. It's my nature to feel for something, and if possible, save it."

"But don't you feel the scorpion stinging you?"

"What can I do? That is its nature. I can't change it. And in the same way, you can't change my nature."

He didn't hate the scorpion for stinging him because he understood its nature. Even if you are stung sometimes, keep on giving.

Even if you quarrel at home, set good examples through giving and involvement in Yoga. Make the other realize the benefits by your own life. If that fails and your partner won't recognize the benefits, there's no point in your living together with negative feelings. Mutual understanding brought you together. If the minds don't agree, why stay together fighting constantly?

After all, what is marriage? Marriage doesn't simply mean signing a piece of paper. If you have different goals, you are not married. You must have one aim in life—two bodies, but one mind, like two wings of the same bird or two oars of the same boat. If that is not there, and there are no children whose growth you might hurt by separation, then talk it over and in a friendly way say, "We seem to have different goals in life. You're interested in that, so go experience it; let me experience this."

There's nothing wrong in it. There's no bondage that requires you to be together when the goal is not the same. But first try to come together by inspiring the other. If everything fails, your conscience can say, "Yes, I tried my best." If you know you can't do anything more, save your soul first.

However, when children are involved, I don't condone breaking up the marriage. If you love your children, stay together—at least until the children are grown. Until the job of raising your children is over, you have a contract. The children—not the courts—should be old enough to sanction your divorce. At the same time, if you're really having constant trouble together—which will make the children unhappy—then sometimes it might be better to part. But know that you really cannot replace the mother and the father, and it will be a setback in the mind of the child.

Don't think that just because your aims are different you always have to run for a divorce. You can talk it over. The fact that you are still together means there is still love for each other, but your interests may now be different. If that is so, peacefully talk and say, "Okay, temporarily we will stay away from each other." Many problems are solved with time if you stay apart for a period, because sometimes when you are constantly facing each other every trifling thing creates more tension. A temporary separation will calm things down. You will have the opportunity to think of all the nice things you both were enjoying, and the rift will heal.

Don't forget that marriage is for giving, not for getting. It is a path of quick growth to realize God. Whether you are a monk or a businessman, a doctor, a poet, or a lover, you can lead a spiritual life by dedicating your life. If you are dedicated to your wife, to your family, you are a dedicated person. Don't constantly demand things from your family members. You do not have a family for your own pleasure, but to serve them all. If you are a husband, you should think of yourself as the servant of the wife. You are the caretaker and the custodian of the wife. If you are the wife, you should think you are the maid of the husband.

But instead it seems we always demand: "I'm your husband. I must have this," or "I'm your wife; you must give me that." Is it for that sake that you married? To get? No, it was to give.

34. Sex

Every particle is a magnet. Even an atom has positive and negative charges, a north and a south pole. A powerful magnet means powerful current. The powerful magnet retains its power because it doesn't lose its magnetism. The human body is also a magnet. Through proper living you can retain magnetism in your body—which is expressed as dynamic personality. If you reserve your energy and are careful not to dissipate it unnecessarily, you will become a powerful magnet. The ability to do this is available to everyone. It's your birthright.

Be aware of the vitality you spend in your actions. According to Yogic scriptures, it requires sixty morsels of food to make one drop of blood, and sixty drops of blood to make one drop of semen. If you conserve that, you gain vitality. The more you save, the more you benefit. When conserved and properly transformed, seminal energy gives you an aura of vitality. That energy is suffused through the body which begins to glow. You may sometimes see the astral body around such a person. This aura shows the purity and beauty of mind. Anyone who preserves this vital energy will have that glow, or personal magnetism. They won't need make-up to attract others; all they have to do is make up their minds not to lose their energy. Moderate or occasional sex spends only a portion of your vital energy and is easily replaced.

There's no sin in sex. Pleasure between the two sexes is good, it's part of nature. God created that inclination. If there is sin, it's overindulging. In Yoga the key is moderation in thought, word, and deed—which includes sex. Beyond limitation, even nectar becomes poison. Enjoy life well, but don't get entangled. To enjoy life, you must have some limitation. Sometimes people understand and think Yoga advocates no sex. That is not so. Yoga teaches the middle path. Yoga is not for the person who never sleeps or always sleeps, nor for the one who always fasts or always feasts. On the middle path, you'll really enjoy yourself. If you don't eat from morning until noon, you'll surely enjoy your lunch. But if you keep on nibbling, you won't enjoy the meal.

It's the same with sex. When done well, it becomes divine. In family life sex can become a kind of service or ceremony. The family people who live a beautiful life of service to each other and the world at large, won't lose anything from that union. Of course, at the same time they can't live like monks—without personal responsibilities.

Many priests, nuns, and monks take vows of celibacy. Normally that is understood to mean abstaining from any sexual act. But in Yoga celibacy is not practiced simply to conserve seminal energy. Priestly celibacy frees these people from personal obligation, which helps them remain completely neutral and thus better able to serve everyone without any partiality. Yoga monks automatically become celibate when they have a thirst to know the Absolute God, and feel that in order to do so they must rise above the physical body and the senses. They don't push down the sexual thirst and walk over it—sexual repression is dangerous. Rather, they are people who are totally interested in God and don't take time to think of anything else.

Marriage helps in limiting sex. If you have sexual desire which you find doesn't dissolve simply by your thinking, then you should find a partner with the same goals and marry each other. Of course, you can still have sex and babies without marriage and legal papers. But if you publicly say, "She is my girl, I am married to her," and she says the same, it helps. If you don't do that, you may go with one person one day, with another the next, and still another on the third day. You will have no limitations. Your mind will run away constantly seeking more experiences.

Publicly taking a marriage vow forces your own pride to help you avoid overindulgence.

There's no sin in homosexuality. It doesn't hurt anybody. Both partners are happy. They just play. It isn't even going to harm any of the internal organs like smoking and drinking do. Smoking cigarettes is worse than homosexuality. If that is a sin, then giving a rubber pacifier to a baby for gratification is a worse sin.

But homosexuality is a sort of one-sided fixation, perhaps caused by being too close to the mother or the father and later not wanting to see the opposite sex. Lasting sexual joy naturally occurs between positive and negative. It's nature's way. Homosexuality, like masturbation, is a form of mental bondage. And it can be changed—not by worrying about the problem, but by driving better ideas in which drive the old ones out. Just as an auto mechanic gets rid of the old grease by shooting in some clean grease, the mind can put new fixations in to force the old ones out.

Wet dreams also come from the mind. If the mind understands the situation, you can easily avoid anything. But if the mind is always after something and you can't satisfy it physically on the waking level, then the mind will go after it on the dreaming level. When the mind wants satisfaction and the physical body refuses to co-operate, it makes use of the astral body, which is the reason for wet dreams: Physically you are not having sex, but mentally you're after it. That's probably even worse for you than the physical connection you are avoiding. It's like giving more gas while at the same time putting your foot on the brake. You can ruin the engine that way, which is why many people break down. It's better that you sometimes let yourself have something that you are constantly wanting, instead of always physically stopping yourself.

You can also avoid wet dreams by being certain your last meal is well digested before you go to bed. When the stomach is light, you never have heavy dreams or this type of emission. Before you go to sleep avoid reading novels or looking at pictures or TV that will stimulate you, or later while you are sleeping you will try to enact the whole thing within. Watch your mental associations. Before sleeping, wash the body well, change the sheets, and make everything as clean and pure as possible. You can also easily avoid such emissions if you rise between 3:30 and 6:00 A.M. as they usually occur at that time. These are all helpful hints. But know that you may sometimes have an emission without an accompanying dream. If so, there's no harm at all, it's just due to age. It's not exactly seminal fluid. There's no real loss, just forget it.

Don't be frightened of sex. Physical affection is not going to hurt your Yoga practice. As long as you are married you still have certain duties. Don't just repress or refuse the other person. If your partner seems to be demanding too much, you can discuss it. If you want to make some changes in your sexual relationship, they should happen with the understanding and acceptance of both parties. Practice a little give and take, don't hurt the other party.

Until you know you can get along well with each other, don't be in a rush to have children. The world has plenty of children now. You should have an extremely good reason to have a child. Both of you should think you are going to create a wonderful saint. Otherwise, go buy a teddy bear. But if you're not ready for a child, you must use some form of birth control.

The best method of birth control is mind control, but if you can't yet control your mind then some artificial means should be used—though there are probably some afteraffects. Try not to take chemicals that arrest your hormones and gradually affect your system. Use some other method. A diaphragm doesn't poison the system. Even though it's artificial, it's much better than chemicals. But don't feel that by using birth control devices you have full license to overindulge—always be moderate.

There's nothing wrong in physical passion, but it shouldn't only satisfy the flesh. It should be an expression of pure and sincere love within. Otherwise, it's just mechanical and it won't last long—only until the body begins to age a little. Such passion is love with expectation. If you love just for the joy of loving, it won't fall away. You can love anybody and everybody with that pure love. But if you love only waiting for some love in return, in time you will surely be disappointed. Learn to love without trying to always make some kind of bargain out of it.

We don't always have to express our love physically. Of course it's nice to hug and touch each other to show affection, but we can learn to express love in other ways. Over the telephone we don't even see the other person, we only hear their voice and still feel the love. Every action need not end up as physical expression, which often is more gross. We can learn to use more subtle faculties. Sometimes a smile is enough. Train yourself to express love in other ways. Don't always use a pat, a hug, or a kiss. Touching and hugging bring up other urges which you may not want to deal with each time.

We should have a little control. We are not just animals. People go out on dates with each other, they say, because they want to get to know the other person. But one thing leads to another. I usually tell young people that if you want to be pure until you choose the right partner, stay away from all these dates. A few years back many of the youngsters didn't even believe in marriage or in living only with one person. They wanted to date everybody. Now many people are convinced this is not the proper life. I don't tell people to stop doing something, but I do point out how it will affect them. People who keep dating are saying in a way that they want to keep on "trying" somebody out.

Of course you can't just go and give your hand to somebody without knowing him. But knowing is in the mind and the heart. It's like buying an apple—you can go to the shop, pick it up, see it, smell the beautiful aroma, and if the price is suitable, buy it. But you can't bite into it first. There's a limit to knowing. Otherwise you are bitten so many times, that when you decide to give yourself, what will the other person see? A bitten apple. Wait until you know the other's quality and character. See if that one is running after you for your wallet or your beauty. Analyze everything. And if you are really satisfied, then say, "I'm happy. You are the right person for me. Here, I am giving myself to you." That's true matrimonial life.

Try to have that control beforehand. If someone says he just wants to know you better, that is often an excuse to satisfy the senses. Don't play around sexually. It just leads to problems and lots of tension. Sometimes you ruin the life of another person coming to this world. How many unwed mothers and fatherless babies there are already—and abortions. But I feel that if you do become pregnant, it's much better to have the child and give it to an agency for adoption instead of having an abortion.

I know it's difficult in a culture that is constantly tempting you. Life has come to the level of constantly thinking about the physical. Everything is sex or violence—in films, even in advertisements. To sell a muffler or an automobile there is always someone in a bikini, saying, "Buy this now." It's terrible the way sex is used for anything and everything. People are misusing physical beauty. You women who are insisting on equality should not let them do that. They want to sell you. You agree to it when you sell your beauty to them to market their products.

This is not the age of Adam and Eve. Don't be so frank in exposing everything. Women seem to do this more than the men. Unfortunately, Adams are attracted. That's not really your beauty. Let people recognize the beauty of your character. There are thousands of cosmetics that have come to tempt you, cheat you, and live on you. If you stop reaching for cosmetic beauty and instead reveal your cosmic beauty, many of these companies will close. If you model your physical beauty and expose yourself, you create problems. In the *Bhagavad Gita*, Lord Krishna says, "If the womenfolk lose their virtue, the entire culture is gone." Women are the pillars for certain virtues. They are the *shaktis*, the strength.

In this day the women want to do everything, even during the menstrual period when even a touch can rouse all their feelings. At this time the entire body is drained of energy. Glandular changes are occurring and the sex urge is a little more predominant, so it is easy to disturb the physical system. In past ages women were freed from household duties and physical contact with men during this period.

Today people have the same feelings, but they are not so careful. I don't say women should go to such extremes of isolation as in the past, but they can rest and not overdo anything. Sexual relationships also are not advised during that period. It's best to restrict practice of Yoga positions then also.

But don't think Yoga *asanas* and breathing practices will ever adversely affect your sex. Actually these practices are helpful in regulating sexual interest, which at base arises not from the body but from the mind. I recommend the practice of *asanas* so such desires will not always assail you. Instead you can use them whenever you want. Sexual hunger is like any other natural thing. When you are hungry, you eat. When you feel sleepy, you sleep. Overindulgence is the only thing to avoid; as a Yogi you can have better control over your sexual life.

35. Child-Parent Relationships

Tamil scriptures say the best gift that children can give to their parents is to excel them. The parents who have truly devoted children are fortunate. What other wealth could they want? According to the poet-sage Thiruvallavar, the parents' duty is to raise their children with such high standards that at any gathering the children are asked to take the foremost place where they can pass on beautiful thoughts to others.

Parents must see that their children receive the knowledge to be good people and leaders. If they really love their children, they will show them the way. In return, children have the duty to bring admiration to their parents. People should say, "What great prayer and penance the parents must have performed to raise such a child as this." Through the children, the mother and father are praised.

It's not easy to raise a child. Giving children right knowledge is more important than all the material comforts. They need to know how to live a life of joy and peace. That's what the parents should give—not just things to make them soft or fat. Parents should pass on the knowledge gained through their own life experiences. Sharing this basic knowledge is certainly more useful than all the luxuries.

How many children are spoiled with credit cards? Their parents give them money and big cars when the children don't even know where they are going or what they are doing. Maybe they employed one or two servants to take care of the child when it came, and later gave material comforts: fine clothes and all the pocket money they wanted. That's no way to teach children. When they are inexperienced and still learning, they should not be allowed the freedom to accumulate all kinds of difficulties. So-called "free" children are later stranded and can't find their way out of confusion. Only through real understanding will they learn to live peacefully. To train the child properly, parents should be loving, but strict and firm.

Competition between children is also not healthy. School systems err when they force children to compete for grades. That's not teaching individuals. Teachers should know each student and teach accordingly. Giving grades causes many disappointments, anxieties, and tensions. Some children have even committed suicide because of a bad grade. Competition often begins at home by comparing one child with another or getting one to do something by offering candy or something—like bait for an animal. Children shouldn't be treated that way.

Instead, treat each child at his own level. Give him confidence. Show him that life's games are playful, not really to win over the other person. Otherwise you create rivalry and jealousy. Teach in a gentle way. You can always say, "You are wonderful as you are. That's great. You don't have to copy the other person."

Children raised in a competitive environment are still searching for peace. Those given all the material comforts soon know this hasn't made them tranquil. Many of them are unhappy and searching everywhere. So many parents lament that their children go after drugs or other religious beliefs. But they don't realize that the love they have given through material possessions didn't reflect the proper understanding. The children are still after what they didn't find at home.

What is the purpose of using drugs? At one time many young people thought—and some still do—that by drugs they could find that peace or tranquility. Their motivation was genuine. They said, "I want to be high," which really meant they wanted to experience tranquility. But, unfortunately, in this space age people want everything quickly. They won't wait for anything. In the West particularly, it's fast communications, fast traveling, fast cooking, and fast eating. People won't even take the time to cook gently by putting the firewood on the fire a piece at a time.

That's all past. Now it's buy a packet, drop it into boiling water, take it out, and eat—finished! Probably even the packet itself is edible. Everything is so fast: instant tea, instant coffee, instant breakfast. Why not instant *samadhi?*

Naturally, that's what they wanted, to bring on that instant tranquility. They heard about the drugs and they innocently wanted to try, not knowing it was going to disturb them. They were just interested in that peace. But many of them are intelligent people. When they found that it was not going to be lasting and genuine they dropped it. They did so because of their own conviction, not because of some government laws; no laws could have stopped them.

Many have also turned to Eastern religious beliefs for the same reasons—looking for that peace. Actually there's nothing new in Eastern religions. I'm sorry to say many young people don't seem to be finding tranquility at home. Don't think it's a mistake of their own religion. Usually it's caused by so-called religious teachers—and hypocrisy at home. As they grow today, children see constant fighting between different religions—even between different denominations in the same religion. People who follow the same prophet or use the same holy book fight with each other. Of course the children are puzzled, "What is this? They talk about God, yet they fight with each other. If their talk of holiness, religion, and God is going to end up in more fighting, then we don't want it any more." If more lives are destroyed in the name of religion and God than by other wars, can we blame the children for not wanting that kind of religion? We have failed to set better examples for them.

As parents we may follow Jesus or Moses. But after going to the church or synagogue, we come back and do things contrary to their very teachings—by black marketing, exploiting, and not treating people equally by dividing them in the name of race, religion, color, community, or caste. If we say at worship that there is only one Father in heaven and we are all His children, and then come home and avoid certain people because we feel they are different, our children see this. And they are very intelligent in this age. "Dad, if that is what you do in the name of religion, why do you want me to follow you to church?" They're not hypocrites.

Naturally, if they're disappointed in one thing, they look elsewhere for peace. They shouldn't think that going to the East will be all heaven, or that everyone there is a saint or a Yogi. It's far from that. Every religion has its back door. People are people everywhere. There are both good and bad, evolved and not so evolved. And everywhere—East and West—there are people with universal love. Remember for example, Martin Luther King, who gave his life for a principle, and Mahatma Gandhi.

That's what inspires modern children, and it is one reason we see so many hundreds of thousands of them in Yoga. They are trying to become better people. Yoga is not a religion, but it can help you understand your own religion by showing what is fundamental to all great religions. Many young people who had lost their faith and left their own traditions, went into Yoga and now are returning to their homes, their synagogues, and their churches. They have begun to read their own holy books again. "With Yoga," they say, "I have understood my own religion." In a way it's a master key to open your own religion and reveal its treasures to you. You can use it and open everything with it.

Parents sometimes don't want their children to practice Yoga, but later when they see the beautiful changes happening, they themselves become interested. A girl came to me once and said, "I'm going to California."

"What happened to your college?" I asked her.

"Oh, I'm not interested in that. I just want to go and experience life."

"How will you go there?"

"Well, my parents will get a ticket for me, and they'll give me some money, and I'll go."

"What will you do?"

"I'll just live with my boy friend. I'll live there for two or three months, experience everything."

"Oh, I see, very good, but why did you come to me?" It seems she wanted me to tell her parents who also knew me. I said, "Okay, call them." Right in front of me she called her parents and I said to them, "This is what I have heard from your daughter. That means she doesn't need your advice or experience at home. She just wants to have her own experience. Let her go. But don't give her a ticket or money, not even a cent. Simply ask her to leave right away. Don't even let her come back to your home."

"Is *this* what you are telling them?"

"Well, my child, you don't want their advice. You want your own experience—at their cost. Why should they feed you and give you money? If you want their money, you still need their help and must listen to them. If you don't care, don't take anything."

"I'd better think about this."

"Think well. Where do you want to go and think?"

"Can I come and spend some time at the Ashram?"

"Okay, I'll give you a week."

She came and spent some time at the Ashram, and after a week she said, "I'd like to go and talk to my parents."

"Sure, go." She went back, and that was the end of California. She went back to college, passed with good credentials, and is a wonderful girl.

Parents sometimes need to be strict about such things. If the children no longer want their advice, then there's no responsibility between the parents and the children. But if they still want the money, say, "No. Sorry, we are not going to give it to you so you can go and do anything you want. If you want to experience everything, the door is open. When you get all the experiences, if you want to come back, let us know. You will still be welcome. But we won't give you the money to come back. You will have to come up to the door on your own."

Many children don't like their parents. Maybe they have some good reasons. But no matter how bad the mother or father is, there are still certain duties or debts to repay, because your body was provided by them. In a way, your body belongs to your parents. How many nights your mother kept the vigil, and how many thousands of kicks did she endure while you were in her womb? She couldn't walk or stand too long; her legs swelled. She underwent a lot of pain in child bearing, but she accepted everything to bring a deserving soul here. "There is no temple better than the mother," said the saintly poetess Avaayar. Parents give each child an opportunity to experience life in this body in order to know the truth.

It is true, some parents don't want to have a child, and when it comes they won't even take care of it. They take better care of their plants and their pets than their children. When the child comes they just show it a bottle and won't even give it the milk made for it. The minute God helped the soul come into the womb, even without anyone asking, He also created milk for the child in the mother's breast. The Supreme Mother thinks of everything. As soon as the child comes, the milk is ready. But nowadays, in the name of some modern medicine, the first two or three days the mother's milk is squeezed out. The baby is not allowed to drink it because it is curdled, they say. But that curdled milk is very important. If God wanted the baby to drink other milk, he would have given clean milk immediately. Curdled milk acts as a laxative, which eliminates all the dried fecal matter in the intestines of the child. The first one or two days, the child should drink that milk.

I tell the mothers if you really want to call someone your child, behave like a mother. Don't steal the child's property. The milk belongs to the child—not even to you or your husband. Many mothers refuse to give that milk which God created for the baby because they feel they will lose their beauty. You call that beauty? Who wants your beauty then? That's not beautiful thinking, and it is probably the reason why, after some time, all that they stole from the baby and kept for themselves creates cancer. Denying an innocent baby's property is a sin. Mother Nature knows how to punish. If you violate any of God's laws, you suffer. You can't escape from that. You might escape from man's law, but never God's law. I don't mean to paint a dangerous picture of God. God is not there to punish. But your own mistakes punish you. If you put your finger in the fire, it will burn. You are the cause for your suffering—not God. Don't rob the child of the food God prepared for it. Breast feed.

Unfortunately some parents are selfish, even violent. But as long as the child is still living at their home and being supported by them, then there is still some duty to them. In such homes children should learn to live with their parents by proper understanding. Retaliation just makes things worse. Even if the child may have the ability to teach, it's not easy for parents to learn from their children. Only if they ask the opinion of their children are they open to learn.

If your parents are very selfish, don't even try to advise them. As long as you are taking food, money, and clothes from them, you must listen to them. As long as the child wants the help of the parent, the child-parent relationship is there. But if they continue to obstruct your way and won't allow you to practice anything to improve yourself, or are so attached they won't let you go where you will learn well, then you should consider leaving.

Sometimes parents' love is limited. They won't let their children go away even to study. Those who cry, "You can't leave me or I will die," are not loving parents who think of the child's benefit. They should be willing to let you go, and to see you when you come back. If they won't, why should you be living with them? You don't have to hate them or even dislike them. But if they are not helping in your spiritual growth and are simply attached to you and putting obstructions in your way, go away temporarily. You have no obligation to them. Some scriptures say to treat such parents as your enemy. I don't go to that extreme. But know that though the mother has a claim on your body, she cannot claim your soul. Which is more important to you—your parents or your path? Your first and foremost responsibility is to save your soul.

36. Renunciation

When a person is interested in spiritual life, there is no worldly obligation whatsoever. The world respects Lord Buddha, but he walked out of his palace leaving a beautiful young wife and child, his parents, and his kingdom. Why? There was a higher call. If God calls you at any point, you can leave the world. All your obligations are finished because you are going to become a better child of God, so you can help not only one family, but thousands of other families afterwards. The sincere seeker is like a man whose head is on fire and is running for water. Nobody can stop him.

The only way to be happy is to dedicate yourself completely to God or all of humanity. Live to bring peace and joy to everybody. This is the only way to true happiness. There are no shortcuts. Kapilar, a great and ancient sage whose works are found in Tamil literature, says: "Do one thing at a time, and let that one thing be only good. And do that one thing right away. Do not postpone it until tomorrow." This minute! Why? If you always say, "Tomorrow, tomorrow," you don't know when death will come. When he comes you can't send him away with praise, "Oh, you're wonderful. I heard a lot about you, sir." You can't escape like that, or write a big check and say, "Take it, man. Come another time." You can't even get a substitute; "See that eighty-five-year-old man there always coughing and sneezing? He's actually waiting for you. Why don't you go to him?"

"I came for you and you only."

These teachings of the saints create dispassion in us because we tend to think we have a lot of time to do everything "tomorrow." Where is that tomorrow? Who has guaranteed it? Every minute we die. Only by His grace does our breath come back in. When that stops, it's the end. So make hay while the sun shines. Today we have health, energy, interest, and places to practice spiritual disciplines. We have guidance. We should use that because nobody knows what will happen tomorrow.

The Hindu scriptures say that a man can have three supreme gifts: a human birth, which is very rare; a thirst to know the truth; and a spiritual guide to show the way. Whoever has all three is most fortunate. Many have human birth but have neither the urge to know the truth nor the guidance. Some people may have the urge to know but have no one to show them. Some have the guidance available but no inclination to know. Ask yourself what you have. If you have all three, are you enjoying the benefit? Question yourself. If you get the right answer, you are fortunate. Otherwise, you are just wasting your time.

Even if your dedication is not a hundred per cent at first, some dedication will lead to more. But if you want permanent peace, you will want to lead a dedicated life, constantly living for the sake of others. Then nobody can disturb your peace. That sacrifice is the key to peace, and without peace there's no joy or happiness.

In some way or another we must renounce. The renunciate is not a loser, but a gainer. Instead of belonging just to one fenced-in area, he belongs to the world. If he renounces his little home, that doesn't mean he must leave it, but that he has broken the fence around the place he called home. Now he belongs to everybody and everything belongs to him. In fact, he has added to his family. A truly renounced and dedicated person is the emperor of emperors, the king of kings, the richest one in the world. Who is that? The one who possesses nothing. Wanting nothing is to have everything. A person of steady and contented mind will not even desire God. Don't be attached even to God. When you are ready, He will be there with you and in you. You don't need even to want Him.

This is the secret of all religions, the secret of Yoga, and the secret of success. We are all interested in success in life. The secret is not to run after it, then it will come to you.

So eternal joy and immortal peace can be experienced only by renouncing everything and by dedicating everything. This might create a little doubt in people's minds. "What is this renunciation? Should I run away from my home? Where am I to go? A cave? A Yoga ashram?" That is not what is meant. You don't need to run away from anything. Stick to what you are, where you are. Do the same things in the same place but with a different attitude: "I do it for Your sake, not for my own." As things come, let them; the trouble arises when you become attached to them. Even a king in his palace with all his wealth and power can be a renunciate. At the same time the ordinary, humble, so-called seeker in a cave can be attached if he can't let go of his own begging bowl. It's not the things you have around you, but rather what kind of relationship you have with them.

If you renounce all possessions but are still attached to your body, you are not free. Attachment to the body means overindulgence. Too often we see people who misunderstand this, particularly in areas where monk-renunciates live. In India, for example, Vedantic philosophy teaches: "I'm not this body; I'm not this mind. I am that Existence-Knowledge-Bliss Absolute. I am the pure and the auspicious." In that sense we speak of our own true Self, which the scriptures call *Atman* or the image of God.

Hearing that they are not the body or the mind, some Vedantins go to the other extreme from overindulgence and refuse to take care of the body at all. "If I am not the body," they reason, "then why should I worry about it?" They become sick and bony. Many of them end up in hospitals. At one point in his life, Lord Buddha went to the extreme of ignoring the body. One image of Buddha depicts him with all his ribs sticking out. Then he realized that without the body nothing can be achieved. The body is the necessary vehicle through which we can even experience absolute bliss. It is given to us by God.

The body, senses, and the world are for experience. You don't have to renounce the world. A true Yogi or spiritual person will be in the world, enjoying it well—but not in the normal sense.

Enjoyment is not just sensual. Enjoyment means using things well without being affected by them. Be in the world but don't get caught in it.

The experience is like that of a boat in water. The boat is in the water but the water is not in the boat. If the boat just floats in the water, it cannot only save itself, but it can also take others from shore to shore. But if it chums up with the water and says, "Come on in and join me," then it won't be able to save others, nor will it be able even to save itself. It will just sink.

People should learn how to live in the world as a boat floating on the water, so they can save themselves and also help others. That's a renunciate's life. How can you live in this world without getting caught? Through total detachment—having no personal desires for things—just use what comes for the benefit of humanity. Whatever your position in life, you can learn to be that renunciate. You don't need to leave anything. Just have that detached attitude in life, and perform everything as your duty.

You can live this way in family life, fulfilling your duties without a possessive attitude. You are the servant of your partner; the children who come are God's children. You can feel: "God wants me to take care of a few people. I accept it without attachment. A saintly householder will not see his children and his neighbor's children differently. He will see that his first responsibility to his immediate family is carried out before other responsibilities and service. Thereafter, he will always check to see who needs his service most. He will have that neutral vision. With the right partner you can be a renounced person in the midst of married life.

Some people choose to become monks. They renounce their personal lives completely because they are interested in serving humanity without dividing their lives into personal and public responsibilities. They choose not to marry in order to be totally free from all personal liabilities.

Sometimes priests, thinking of leaving the church and getting married, come to me for advice. I explain that if their interest is to serve humanity without the limitations that are part of family life, then they shouldn't marry. If you want to serve everybody at all times, then don't have anybody as your own. Many of these people have said to me, "We never heard this kind of explanation before. We just hear 'the Vatican said so.'" "In the Vatican,"

I said, "you must convince people, instead of saying, 'If you don't do it, we'll fire a cannon at you.'" In Yoga there is no canon law. If you like it, take it. If you don't like it, try another way. Many priests who heard these explanations went back to the church.

It is difficult to be totally neutral if you have personal responsibilities foremost in mind. That's why doctors won't operate on their own wives or children. Imagine a married monk in charge of an orphanage with forty children. A wealthy man comes and gives some nice clothes, a little money, and some sweets. At the same time the monk's own children don't have enough food or clothes. Naturally the father will have the tendency to take a little for his own children first. But monks are beyond all personal limitations and associations. They are not truly renounced unless they are even free from attachment to the order or yoga institute where they live. Even then they are perfectly free to become householders if they choose.

In some cases, people finish their student life and don't feel like becoming householders. They're just not interested in marriage and family. They feel that sometime back they exhausted that or experienced it fully. By nature they are not inclined toward that any longer. It's not that they push it away, but that it leaves them. Then they wonder, "What am I going to do married? There's nothing there for me to enjoy. I don't seem to have any interest in it." In that case they can go directly to the life of the renunciate. It's not that they renounce these things, because if they try, these things will simply wait to catch them later.

That's escaping. If you are running from something or pushing it aside, it will say, "Aha, you are pushing me out. Okay, I'll wait at the door. When you are a little weak, I'll run and catch you." Real renunciation comes naturally. Instead of you dropping out, all your other desires just drop from you. For example, when the fruit is still green, it clings to the tree. If you try to pull it off, it refuses to come, which means it's not ripe—it still wants to be with the tree. Imagine then that you are a fruit like that. As long as you are green, you will want to cling to the tree of life. You can't jump off; you shouldn't even allow someone else to pull you away. If by chance you are pulled, you bleed and it hurts. Even if you allow someone to pull you away, you are not fit to eat. You will have to be artificially ripened, and lose most of your natural flavor.

Stick to the tree. Gather all the nourishment you can get there because the tree of life is there to give you all experiences. When you get everything and when you are really ready, you will say, "I'm ripe now, so why should I stick around here?" Even before you think of it, you drop off. The tree says, "Now you are fully ripe; don't cling to me. Get out!" Instead of you pushing the tree, the tree has pushed you out. Then you are a drop-out from the tree of life.

That's real renunciation. Such a person need never fear falling back into it all again. But if you come away prematurely or as an escape, you will constantly fear life, and worry: "Will that tree draw me back again because I got away?"

On occasion I welcome people who come forward to embrace the order of *Sannyas* or renunciation. They come to renounce everything that would disturb their peace. They come to retain that peace, to establish it, and then to serve others by helping them find that peace. If they want total liberation, they must renounce not only their errors but also their merits. If that is their temperament, it will come automatically. The only thing they must remember from then on is not to do anything for themselves. They are renouncing all selfishness—all personal interests. To prepare the mind for selflessness, they practice these techniques: meditation, mantra repetition, sense control, good diet, *asanas, pranayama*, devotional chanting, selfless action, study, and reflection. Once they achieve peace, serenity, purity, and a relaxed state, they are totally free from egoism. They are totally dedicated, eating, breathing, and living for the sake of others. Their very existence is for others. That total renunciation.

Often renunciation happens without plan. In my childhood I recognized that my life seemed to be guided by some unseen force. I feel that way even today. People sometimes ask me, "How did you get into the spiritual field? How did you become a Swami?" which is a name for a monk. It's like asking, "How did you come into this world?" I can't take credit for anything, for what I am now or what I will be tomorrow. I don't think I consciously worked for it.

From my childhood I was told by my mother that I was even born because of her spiritual practices, which is probably the reason I more or less transferred from so-called worldly activities —schooling and business—to the spiritual field and became a renunciate. My mother was sad and asked, "Why should you leave us? Why can't you remain here and still do whatever you want?"

"Mama, I really wanted to do that. But somehow you spoiled the entire thing."

"Why?"

"You probably wanted a child like this or you shouldn't have gotten initiations and followed monks and wished for a son like that."

Our home was more or less an open house for any passing spiritual seeker. In a way, it is my parents who caused me to be here. My father always wanted great men in every field to come and spend time in our home. There was always someone visiting and living in one section of the home; an astrologer, a philosopher, a poet, or a Swami. We children learned by example.

If there are one or two older brothers or sisters in your family, you can easily say, "They are there to take care of you." Fortunately for me, I had an older brother, and I told my parents, "He will take care of everything." After a long time my father wrote a letter to me saying, "I just heard a lecture where the father had two children—one to make him happy while living in this world, the other to make him happy after he dies. I am fortunate in having these two children. Even after my death you are going to make my soul happy." I still have that letter. His words have helped me a lot. I think it's my father's greatness that brought me to this service. If your parents have that kind of beautiful understanding, then you are truly fortunate.

PART V:

BACK TO THE SOURCE

37. Life and Death

Life itself is a game, but to enjoy it you should know the rules. You might go with a group to the playground to play soccer. Out of that group of fifty or sixty, twenty-two people come forward. Already there are two groups: one to watch, another to play. And in order to play the game they must divide again into two smaller groups, eleven for each team. Moreover, all eleven cannot play the game the same way. One is made to stand between the two poles. You call him the goalkeeper. His aim is to keep the others from scoring. So you displace people from each other —separate them.

You get the point? They are separated purposely. You all went as one group, but you want to play. You can't play as one group. You separate people and make them stand in different places. You make some rules: The goalkeeper can touch the ball with his hands; no one else can.

He's not unique—that is the game, those are the rules. We have a set of rules to play the game. Only then can we start kicking the ball. Within these rules we play the game, but without missing the idea that we are all playing, not fighting. We purposefully separate ourselves to play. Playing is unity. Different positions and different ways of playing are diversity. But if people miss that unity in the playing, and instead of kicking the ball kick each other, the umpire calls a foul.

In life we do the same thing. We are all playboys and playgirls. Yes, literally we are playing. There is one umpire. His empire is everywhere. He is just watching. He doesn't stop us immediately for our foul plays. He just notes them. But at the end of the game he may put us to shame. He may even put us out of the game—boxed, nailed, and buried.

There are some rules to this game of life. You have your freedom, but if you take unlimited freedom, you'll mess up the whole game. Your freedom should not affect the other person's freedom. Once in Sri Lanka I was driving from Kandy to Colombo. While I was en route, it was announced Sri Lanka had just won her freedom, and the politicians told everyone, "We are all rulers of this country now. This is everyone's kingdom."

People thought, "We are the rulers of our own kingdom." Unfortunately that was misinterpreted by many. They thought they could do anything they wanted. To enjoy the new freedom of their country, I saw a few people sitting right in the middle of the road playing cards. I stopped the car and asked, "What are you doing?"

"We are the kings of our country. We have the freedom to do anything."

"Oh, I see. All have freedom?"

"Yes, sure."

"Do I also have the same freedom?"

"Sure. You are one of us."

"Okay. My freedom is to drive over you. Shall I do that? You have the freedom to play. I have the freedom to drive."

That's where people miss the point. Freedom is not only for you, it's for everybody. We should all live in harmony without affecting the other person's freedom. That's the reality behind the unreal world. We must co-operate with each other.

Always think big. We are not just tiny little dots. We belong to the whole universe; we are part of the whole. We could never survive if we separated ourselves completely. The toe has a different name and shape than the hand or the head, but all are parts of the whole body.

We're all cells of the Cosmic Body. If one cell gets hurt, its infection will slowly spread into other areas of the world. We can't simply ignore it, thinking, "Well, I'm all right and happy. The problem is somewhere in that farthest corner." The farthest corner is like your toe. What if your brain says, "I'm six feet high. I don't need to worry about that. It's somewhere way down there on earth." If the brain and eyes ignore the wound, they will soon see how quickly poison comes to the head.

So when there's a problem, the eyes should immediately examine it. The hands should go to help. The brain should think of ways and means to clean it—because we belong to the whole body. This feeling of wholeness is what you call holy. The one who feels he is just part of the whole will just give and give and give. And the more he gives, the more he gets from the others.

Our separate individualities are just to help us play and enjoy the game. At base we are all the one whole, the Self, which is infinitely joyous. We are that infinite joy. We're not unhappy little creatures, we're always joyful, always peaceful, never changing, never moving. That is our own true nature. What is it that changes, gets disturbed and excited? The mind. The mind minds its business. Why should we worry about it? Realize that what is mortal is the mind and body. Mortality means changing. Actually, nothing can die in this world. We can never destroy. The *Gita* says, "One that is—is always. And one that is not, never is."

Then what is the meaning of death? One form dies to give room to another form. It is death for this form and birth for that form. A piece of material dies, a nice shirt is born. A log of wood is dead and gone, but you see some beautiful furniture in the home. That's death. The essence is always there.

The world is nothing but name and form. We constantly change the name; we change the form. A boy is dead; an adult is born. The adult is dead; papa is born. Papa is dead; grandpa is born. Grandpa is dead; the dead body is born. He is dead, but "it" is here. If he is dead and gone, where is "it" lying? The immortal one can never be mortal. If it's sometimes mortal and sometimes immortal, it's not really immortal. The one that is appears to be many.

You see the same principle when a small seed is gone or dead but the tree is present. Then the tree is dead and the log is here. What is mortal will always change. Death is inevitable. All who are born have to die one day. We have to allow nature to take its course. But we need not feel the loss. One discards his body because it's old or it's no longer fit for use. The soul continues on to another body, which may or may not be physical.

The soul continues its journey by changing vehicles. Death is just like changing an old garment and putting on a new one. Just as you dress the body, the body itself is a cloak for your Self. When it's old you have to change it, so nature gives you something to suit your taste or to fulfill your ambitions and desires. The body you have now is an outcome of your past desires. In your previous birth you had a bundle of desires that could be fulfilled only through this human body.

The soul is always alive. It's immortal. It never dies. Thus, there is no death for us; none of us is really going to die. For the Self there's no incarnation or reincarnation. We are always immortal. We are never dead, and we never have to be reborn. But until we realize that truth we seem to be coming and going all the time. We lived before and we live afterward. However, we do change clothes—the physical bodies.

You may ask, where is the proof? There's a lot of proof, but people don't always want to accept it easily. For example, if a baby born with some disability—a limbless or blind child, one with a tumor, born with suffering—were the first birth of a person, why should God create such suffering for one child and a fine life for another? Both are His children. Is that fun for Him? Can He be all-merciful and still watch a child suffer from its very birth? The child must have lived before and done something for which it is taking the reaction now.

Sometimes you see a born genius, a prodigy. Within two or three years the child plays a musical instrument with great beauty. Or another is an advanced mathematician or can read and write poetry. Where did these children get that knowledge? All of these things prove that their souls lived before. In the case of twins, sometimes you see two completely different temperaments born from the same parents within a few moments of one another.

If you can believe in some life before, why not a life after? Every action has its own reaction. We do so many things now. If we don't face them in this life, we'll face them in a later experience.

We are all just tops spinning about here. But it's the one Player who strings the rope around the tops and spins them. We're all tops being spun with a certain length rope. The length of the rope is our past karma. If our karma is short, we finish our job in just a few rounds and simply sit down.

You are given the body you need to continue toward the goal. If you want to have a nice, fast ride on a highway, you take a good streamlined sports car. If you want to go through the jungle on a dirt road, better trade that car for a jeep. Even a jeep can only go to a certain limit. Then you might have to go on a pony or get down and walk. Different vehicles take you toward the same goal. Which is inferior and which is superior? A sports car, a jeep, a pony, or the legs that carry you? All are equally important. One cannot be useful in the other's place. Your present body is a vehicle that you trade in when it's time to continue with some other vehicle.

If we realize the immortal principle that makes us and shapes us into different forms, why should we be afraid of death? There's no death at all. Just realize: "I'm unborn. I'm undying. I'm in the beginning, I'll be in the end." That means there is no beginning; there is no end. "I am the oldest of the old. Even when the body is dead, I'm not dead. The body changes, but I am constant." All fears are based on the fear of death or losing one's self. If we realize the immortal principle, then there's no fear at all. We can face anything.

38. Prayer

God, anything that is good for me You know. I'm Your child. Guide and direct me. I cannot demand this and that. I may make mistakes by my demands. By my own ego I may do things wrong. So I allow You to work through me.

If you still want to ask for something in prayer, you can say, "Lord, don't you know I'm Yours? Do anything You want. Let me always understand that I am Your child, that You are taking care of me every minute. Give me the boon of always remembering this truth."

God is always there. But you have to reach to receive His help. That's why the Bible says, "Ask and it shall be given." He will not come by force to help you. You must ask for His mercy or blessings. His grace is everywhere. It's not that He selects people and says, "I will bless this one and not that one." He and His creation, which you call nature, are always neutral.

But to become ready to receive His help you need His grace. How can you get it? You must open yourself to Him. He won't force Himself in; He'll wait. Sri Ramakrishna once gave a beautiful example. There were a few fishermen preparing to go to sea early in the morning. Within half an hour they were ready and all the boats were sailing out—except one.

That one man complained, "What's this? My boat's not moving. All the others seem to be sailing fine. The wind seems to be partial. It gives its force to those boats but not to mine. How could this be?"

He was blaming the wind when a person standing on the shore called to him, "Say, what is this? They have all unfurled their sails, caught the wind and are going. But you haven't opened your sails."

"Oh, I see. I'll do that." He opened his sail and immediately the boat went forward, and then stopped. He stood up and shouted, "See, I told you. He is not impartial. I think He has some kind of grievance against me. You said for me to open my sail. I did that and it moved a little, but now I'm stuck again. What can I do now?"

"Friend, you are quick to blame others. You don't want to see your mistake. Did you pull up your anchor?"

"Ahhh. I see. I'm terribly sorry." And the minute he did, he sailed on.

God is like that. He wants to bless you, but He can't force Himself in. He waits for you to be ready, for you to ask, to open your mind. That's why the scripture says that even a camel can pass through the eye of a needle before God can come into the millionaire's mind. Those are not the exact words, but you probably understand. Does it mean God is so weak he does not have the capacity to come into anyone's mind? No, He wants to go there, but there's no room. There's just room for autos, radios, TV, money, estates—no room for Him.

A poor man has nothing. It's all vacant. So God comes and enjoys the space. If God wants to come in, make room. The devotee should aspire to this. If he is sincere, he might feel he is so weak he cannot even ask for blessings. Then he asks indirectly, "Lord, by myself I have no capacity to ask anything of You. Without Your blessing and Your grace, I cannot even pray." This itself is a prayer. He becomes aware of his smallness, which opens up his mind.

This open-mindedness means you are spreading your heart, opening up your safe. By prayer and meditation—by asking in this way—you open. But at the same time you must do something else. Remember the fisherman who opened his sail, but still did not move. There are many people who from childhood go to church and regularly pray but still won't change their ways. They continue to reveal their vicious side.

They may be doing what's given in scripture, but unfortunately they haven't pulled up the anchor. They are tied down to the world by so many ropes. That's why you need both discrimination and dispassion—they go together. On one side you cut all the ties that bind you into the world; on the other, you open your heart to God. Only then can you sail. This is why scriptures say you must give everything to God. Don't keep yourself tied to petty things. Then in your very asking you feel His grace; otherwise God is just there. You have to do your part. God helps those who help themselves. Ramakrishna says, if you walk one foot toward God, He is merciful and runs ten feet toward you. But if you don't walk that one foot—no, don't use your calculator and think He will come eight feet. *You* have to begin the process.

When you worship are you making contact with the main battery which is God? Through your prayer and devotion you should be in communication with God. You make a connection. Suppose you are a bulb connected to a battery with a wire. If there is a loose connection, you won't receive the light. If you are the bulb trying to get light from the charged battery, or the image of God, your prayer is the connecting wire. If the prayer is a loose connection, you won't get the light.

Do you get my point? Many people just utter their prayers: "Oh God, bless me. Help me. I believe in You with full faith; Nobody else can help me—yes, yes, Mr. So-and-so. I'll finish my prayer and come soon." They repeat their prayers while their eyes roll around looking at people. "How many are here? Where is that friend? Did he come?" Of course, that prayer is just lip service. "I am Thine. All is Thine. Let Thy will be done"—while one hand is holding the wallet in the pocket. Such prayer has a bad connection. When you pray you have to forget everything else.

Even if you know the entire scriptures by heart and can recite them backward from the last page to the first, you will not gain God's grace. He doesn't want your scholarly attitude or your literacy. He doesn't bother about how much you know. He wants to know how much you practice. Flowery words and lengthy prayers are not that important. It must come from the heart, if only a single word—even a meaningless word. Many children communicate with their mothers this way, by a sound no one else understands. When the baby cries a certain way, only the mother understands because there's a special language.

In the same way, the ultimate, absolute Mother knows, even without your words. Just feel; She knows. It's the feeling. The heart must pray, not the lips, not the head. That's very important in devotion. Always develop the heart. Whatever you do, wherever you go—whether it's temple, church, mosque, or synagogue, prostrations or liturgy—let the heart always be there. The sacred heart is a secret heart. You need not expose it or show it to others. Just let Him know. Let it be secret communication.

That's *sattvic* devotion. Such people who have that way of devotion are fortunate. It's of great value. We all have that in us, but unfortunately our intelligence tends to take over too often. Just allow the heart to melt. It's the easiest way to approach Him. Become a baby in the arms of the Mother. One sage used to say, "Lord, I know the trick. I don't need to read anything. I don't need to do anything. I just cry. I know I'll get you." There are some people who begin to cry the moment they begin praying. It's the best way to get His light.

We are each of us like light bulbs. Unless the connection is well made through the heart, we won't draw His current and we won't get the enlightenment. The positive and negative must also be separated, the giving and the taking. Unless you give well, you can't take well. Just give for the sake of giving and the taking will come automatically. Current runs one way and then comes back. If you try to do business all the time—"I am giving so much; I should be getting so much"—it causes a short circuit, which creates heat or tension.

So, no loose circuits; no loose connections. The amount of current you can receive also depends on the filament in the bulb. The only difference between a 6-watt bulb and a 1,000-watt bulb is the size of the filament. The current and connection are the same, but the bulb with a greater filament draws more energy. The filament is your mind. If you are narrow-minded, you can only receive a little of God's grace. Widen your mind and your filament is wider; you get a lot of grace and you shine more. Unfortunately, many bulbs do not have a filament at all. They make connections but they never glow. You need a clean mind and a broad mind. But at the same time, don't be greedy. What will happen if the bulb is made for 110 volts and you draw 220? The bulb will fuse. Just try for your limit. That's why the devotee says, "Lord, I'm not going to ask you to give me this and that. I might be greedy. If you start giving me all I want, I might get fused. So You decide what to give me, how to give it to me, and how much to give me. I am just here."

God knows all languages. Just pray in your mother tongue. When you sing or pray to God from your very heart you won't have to worry if you hit the right note or not. Sincere and wholehearted prayer is meditation. You are one-pointed with your attention. When you focus your mind on a particular idea connected with God, then prayer is a form of meditation. The Gayatri mantra given to renunciates is also a prayer. Its meaning is: "Lord, who is enlightening the whole cosmos, enlighten my intellect also." Think of the meaning and repeat it.

In meditation you focus your mind on a prayer, a mantra, your own breathing, or on the heart beat. When you meditate on the heart, imagine that God is there making your heart beat. He Himself is the beat. It is His movement within you. That's what Hindus call the Dancing of *Nataraja*.

Choose what you like for meditation or prayer, but mean what you say and what you do. When the thinking-speaking-acting all go together, then they will bear fruit. When I speak, my hands move this way and that without my consciously willing it. Without my knowledge my body automatically co-operates, helping me to express something. Mental expression is foremost; the body will act accordingly.

The same thing happens with your prayers and daily actions. Prayers transform themselves into actions. Actions offered up are prayers. In time every action is a prayer; it's a meditation. You won't be able to live any other way. In the beginning you may be able to separate them: "This is action and this is prayer." It's a good way to start. Set time for one and the other. But gradually it expands until the prayerful attitude pervades your entire life. In the end everything is prayer.

39. *If You Tune, You Get the Music*

One fine morning when his consort Maha Lakshmi was busy in the kitchen, Lord Narayana opened a safe deposit box in his palace and took out a small box. He opened it and was looking inside appreciatively with great feeling and devotion. When you respect something very much you put it near the eyes to see it better, so he was examining it very closely—almost adoring it.

At that moment Lakshmi walked into the room. Immediately, Narayana closed the box and put it behind his back. Of course she became inquisitive and asked. "What's the secret? Is it a photograph of somebody? What is it? I must see it."

"No, no, no. It's nothing, honey."

"Oh, I must see it and know what it is. You can't have any secrets from me."

"No, no, no."

"We are living together. You are for me. I am for you. How could I have any secrets without your knowing, or you without my knowing? You must show me!"

"Please, let me have at least something special for my . . ."

"No, I can't let you."

"You must—" But she was at liberty to reach with her hand and take the small box from him. Then she opened it and looked inside. But she couldn't see anything, just an empty box. She looked back at him, questioning.

"Look very carefully."

"It's just an old box with some dust in it." She leaned closer to blow it away.

"Oh, don't do that! Don't blow it out."

"What is it! Why are you like this? It's just an empty box with some dust."

Then he whispered: "It is the dust from my devotees' feet."

The Lord worshipping dust from His devotees' feet? Then who is greater? It's easy to rise and be this and that, but very difficult to become dust. But in the spiritual sense, it's a must.

During the last century there lived in South India a great singer-saint by the name Tyagaraja. *Tyaga* means dedication. *Raja* means king, which is another aspect of God. God is the greatest dedicater. He does everything for our sake; nothing for Himself. He is the king of dedication. Later on they called this saint, Tyagabrahman. *Brahman* is another name for the Absolute Almighty. This man was considered the most dedicated person because he lived in God always.

He saw God. He was speaking to Him, sometimes teasing Him, he was that close. You can't imagine what his songs were like. Such songs can't be composed just from intelligence. They are so beautiful. He was a great devotee of the Lord in the form of Sri Rama. In one of his songs, he addresses Sita, the consort of Rama, and says: "Ah, do you think by your beauty and love you can hold Him with you and keep Him from coming to me? I am not a great person, but my love is greater than yours. You can't keep Him away from me."

Once he said: "Hey, Rama"—He would call Him just like that —"How tasty and sweet is Your name. Your name is sweeter than You." Yes, the names of God are sweeter than God Himself. You can't taste God, but you can taste His name. If we just repeat the name, within a few seconds we begin to feel something. Imagine just calling on God: "Hey, Rama; Hey, Siva; Hey, Allah; Hey, Christ." It sounds a little familiar. Only the sincere devotee can come so close. They are all sweet names. We can melt by repeating God's name. That's the power of repeating the name.

The Lord cannot give Himself directly. It's like the dynamic power of all the electricity, millions of kilowatts which cannot come to our home directly. If by chance it does, our home won't be there and we won't be either. So out of His greatness and His love to serve us, He limits Himself, and steps Himself down by transformers, as it were, to come to us usefully. Knowing our limitations, He comes down through the Word, the holy names, which we can repeat and taste the bliss. The more we chant, or praise His name, or repeat it, the more we go into ecstasy.

That's why Tyagaraja says, "Rama, Your name is so sweet." He can't even say how sweet. That's the greatness of singing the Lord's name, which is part of the devotional path known as Bhakti Yoga. Devotion is more developed, and expressed by singing His glory, by constantly repeating His name. You live in Him and He lives in you. This is an important practice for developing devotion. God says, "The devoted ones are near to Me, because they love Me more." If you love Him more, you draw Him more. If you tune, you get the music. Chanting songs or psalms composed of God's holy name is not just an appealing prayer or asking for something. The vibrations of your song elevate you to another plane. Every cell of your body will vibrate on that divine level. You repeat God's name; you become God. You sing and dance in ecstasy. You forget your body; you forget yourself and easily go to that higher level.

Though there are other practices offered in the spiritual field—such as deep meditation, Hatha Yoga *asanas, pranayama,* developing psychic centers, and raising the *kundalini*—they are all rather technical and might be dangerous if they aren't accompanied by much discipline. But there's no danger in singing the glory of the Lord or in chanting or repeating His name. That doesn't require any rigid discipline. If you can't yet discipline your life, that doesn't mean you must stay completely away from spiritual practice. At least do this. Slowly you will get self-discipline.

Bhakti Yoga is really an easy way to practice devotion in these modern times. In past ages it was probably easier to sit and meditate. There was nothing to distract people. But the moment you close your eyes today, a supersonic plane will thunder over your head. Early morning when you sit, here come ten garbage trucks rumbling nearby. You can't do anything. You walk through the streets and there are so many distractions, beautiful things to feed your senses—reading materials and movies just calling to you. Not only is the air polluted nowadays, even the thought forms are polluted. People think in terms of amassing wealth, black marketing, duping, cheating, mugging. In the midst of all this it is very difficult not to be distracted.

If you have an emotional temperament, you like to use your heart. By chanting or repeating God's name, your emotion becomes devotion, and as your love for God develops you come to see and love your Self, which is God and is also your neighbor's Self. So your love for God also becomes love for your neighbor. By this method you develop your ability to love and become more interested in the attributes of God whom you love. You will be interested in reading and studying about the glories of God. That creates awe. And the more you love, the more loveable you become.

The only trouble occurs if we try to limit God, thinking, "This is my God; that is his God." If we think there is only one form or name for God, then we are in trouble. We have to grow universally, without limitations. Of course we love our homes, our countries, our mothers, our religions, but that doesn't mean we should ignore others, or hate them or push them aside. That's limited love. True love of God means universal love.

God created the entire world. All religions say God is the Creator. Each professes that there is only one God. If there is only one God who created the whole world, we are all His children. Suppose a Hindu says, "There is only one God who created all. Then how should I treat a Buddhist, a Catholic, or a Muslim? He is my brother, because my own God, whom I call Father, created him also. So he is the child of my Father."

In a family there may be a child who abuses or scolds the father and even spits in his face. Can one brother say, "That one is not my brother?" Can the father deny him? Even atheists who don't believe in God are still God's children. We are brothers and sisters to them. If we acknowledge one Father for all of us, can we say, "That one is an unbeliever and I hate him. He is not in my family?" Our own Father will not be pleased with that response. As we understand our own religions better, we will have to open our hearts and minds equally to everybody.

40. The Man Who Hated God

If you deny God, you accept Him by your very denial. If you don't believe in Him, why should you deny Him? You have to think of Him even to say, "There is no God." In a way, the one who denies God probably approaches God quickly. Denial is not strong enough—you would have to really hate God. Considering Him your enemy would be your religion. Sometimes you forget your friend, but you don't forget your enemy. You are constantly thinking of him, and that is what the Lord wants: Constantly think of Me. It doesn't matter even if you treat Me as an enemy, but think of Me always.

The story of Prahaladana and his father, Hiranya Kashipu, is proof of this. Hiranya Kashipu was a demonlike man who was a king. He had a young son by name Prahaladana. Since Hiranya Kashipu ruled the entire country he insisted that the teachers in all schools repeat his own name before they began the class. Before any child could start the day, he had to pay respect to the king by saluting his name, "*Om Hiranyaya namah.* Hiranya, I bow before you."

Since the teachers were paid by the king, naturally they felt they had to obey him. But the time came when prince Prahaladana came of school age, and the king sent his son to elementary school. But Prahaladana bore some impressions from the past. A great devotee of God had been born into the family of Hiranya Kashipu which is part of God's playfulness. When the boy went to school, the teacher asked him to say, "*Om Hiranyaya Namah.*"

"What? That's my dad's name."

"Yes, He is supreme for us."

"No, I don't want to say that. I still seem to have in my memory another name, '*Om Namo Narayanaya*' . . ."

"Oh, please don't say that. Your father will kill me. He will think I taught you this. How did you know such a name?"

"Well, all I know is that it is a name of God."

The teacher was very disturbed and ran to Hiranya Kashipu and said, "Sir, oh great Maharaj, your own son is repeating some undesirable name. I taught him to repeat your name, but he didn't want to."

"Bring that fool here." But by the time the child arrived, Hiranya Kashipu had become a little affectionate. "Come, sit here my son. Now what did you say in school?"

"Dad, I just repeated God's name."

"God's name? Who is that God? Don't you know I am the God?"

"No, Dad, you are my dad and I love you. But God is Narayana."

The king couldn't even stand the name. "Child, how did you know this?" He looked fiercely at the teacher who was shivering.

Then a fight began between a true devotee of God and a true enemy of God. No matter how he tried, Hiranya Kashipu couldn't change the mind of the boy, so finally he decided to kill him. But a mysterious power protected Prahaladana. Hiranya Kashipu rolled the child from a mountain top, but the boy came away safely. He tried to have Prahaladana trampled by an elephant, but the elephant came to the child, went around, bowed down, and walked away. The king made the boy's mother give him poison, but when Prahaladana drank the poison he just smiled at his father, it became nectar. Hiranya Kashipu was totally defeated.

He tired and finally said, "All right, where is this dirty Narayana?"

"Dad, He's everywhere."

"He is everywhere? I've been watching for Him for so many years so I could destroy him. You seem to know Him. All right, show me."

"Dad, He is right here—everywhere."

Hiranya Kashipu pointed: "Is He in this pillar?"

"Yes, Dad, He is also in the pillar."

"All right. I am going to kill Him then, right now." Hiranya Kashipu took a sword and struck a great blow on the pillar. Immediately there was an uproar. The pillar split into two halves, and out came the Lord who appeared in a peculiar way as half-man, half-animal, which is called *Narasimha Avatara*. Nara means man. *Simha* means lion.

Why should He appear thus? Because until he acquired all his powers, this same demonic Hiranya Kashipu sometime before had been a very great devotee of God. Then he forgot God and believed that he had become God himself. At one time he had been taught how to repeat a mantra and how to meditate. In time he became a big Yogi, but he practiced with an unclean mind. Whether you are clean or not, if your practice is steady the mantra *shakti* will be attracted to you. Even an impure person can repeat certain mantras and get a certain part of God through the vibrations. God has to come.

So God did come to this man and said, "I am satisfied with your penance and meditation. I have been attracted by you. Ask your boon from Me."

He said, "My request is that I should not be killed at any time by a human being."

"Is that all?"

"No, wait, wait. There's more. I should not be killed by animals."

"Okay."

"I should not be killed by any weapon."

"Okay."

"I should not be killed during the day."

"Okay."

"I should not be killed during the night."

"Okay."

"I should not be killed within the house."

"Okay."

"I should not be killed outside the house."

"Okay."

And after all that he continued, for a demon has little faith, but much fear. "And if by any chance I am killed, from any drop of my blood that falls to the ground, a hundred people like me should come out of that drop of blood."

"Okay." When God promises to give you a boon, He gives you everything. It's up to you to use it or not. Any scientist who probes into matter can discover the atomic force. That great power will not hide from him. But it's up to him to make use of it. How you use the power you acquire from your practices is up to you. Will you make a destructive bomb or a soothing balm? It's the same with the spiritual science. If you practice with a polluted mind, you will receive the power, but you will misuse it to ruin yourself and disturb others. "Are you satisfied?"

Hiranya Kashipu thought a little, and added: "Nor can I ever be killed on the ground or in the sky."

"Okay."

Then Hiranya Kashipu thought, "Now I am going to be immortal. Nobody can kill me." That's why when the pillar opened a half-man, half-lion form came out. It was neither man nor animal. God has His own tricks. He remembered giving the boon that Hiranya Kashipu could not be killed by man or animals, but Hiranya Kashipu never thought of a half-man, half-animal. So He came out in that form. The promise was that he wouldn't be killed by any weapons, nor on the ground, so He immediately grabbed Hiranya Kashipu and placed him in His lap while sitting in the entrance of the house, neither inside nor out, neither on the ground nor in the sky. He used His claws to tear open Hiranya Kashipu's chest, sucked out all the blood, and drank it so not one drop fell. There are terrifying pictures of this with little Prahaladana standing nearby repeating God's name. But the child couldn't see God, only his father dying, and he began crying, "Narayana, I can't see You. What is happening to my dad?" His affection for his father was still there.

And the Lord said, "Child, you still have to grow. You didn't think of Me as much as your father thought of Me."

So an enemy got the vision and visitation of God first; later the devotee. This might be a little puzzling. How can even an enemy of God see God? Whether you are an enemy or a friend, what counts most is the interest—constant remembering. Hating God as his enemy, Hiranya Kashipu always thought about Him. So He appeared. Just at the time of his death, revelation came to Hiranya Kashipu. Before collapsing, he cried, "Lord, please excuse me. What I did is terrible. Forgive me. If I am reborn after this, let me suffer for all these sins, but let me remember You as my good friend. Take my soul away from the body, but give me that boon."

God gave him that. Later Hiranya Kashipu took another birth as a great devotee, lived a long life as a close friend of God, and then passed on.

You may think that all of this is just a nice story. But even if you don't believe the story, at least see the inner meaning. It's very difficult to believe some things. Every scripture has stories with esoteric meaning behind them. You need not believe to the letter exactly what they say. To the intellect it's controversial. All religions have this. But you should understand the inner meaning. Do anything and everything in His name, "All for Siva, all for Vishnu, all for Jehovah, all for Jesus, all for Allah, all for Buddha." That means, "Lord, I follow only you." One-pointed devotion with the entire life dedicated to God is the basic requirement in Bhakti.

That way you lose your individuality—you live for Him and you die for Him. There are many subtle aspects to Bhakti Yoga: personal worship, different types of services before an altar, why we light this or do that, and what the rituals and services symbolize. There is a lot to learn about levels of worship. Such knowledge will come naturally as we continue to grow. Until then let us just be humble, simple, sincere devotees and allow others to be equally good devotees, worshipping the same God through whatever form they choose. Just as five brothers and sisters in the same family have the same father and mother, but like five different kinds of food, so can we all live as one family with our different modes of worship.

That's the essential teaching. We should acquire this ecumenical spirit. Only in this way we can all live together and bring peace and heaven on earth, and through this make our Lord happy.

41. The Ant in the Sugar Hill

There are various approaches to God. Sometimes they seem to contradict each other—one great saint teaches a way that appears to be opposed to another. But if we go to the core of their teachings, we will understand that they are both talking of the same ultimate goal. If two people, A and B, start from the same point, one may walk toward the east, the other toward the west, directly opposite from the other. Suppose they continue on their paths without swerving even a single degree on their compasses. Where will they end up? Face to face. All roads lead to Rome. Any good approach will lead you home. For example, one sage, the great Acharya Shankara, summarized the entire Upanishadic teachings when he said, "The Absolute One is the truth. What you see outside you as its manifestation is not real, but an illusion." When the sage Shankara speaks of *maya* or the illusory world outside, he is not saying that it is not there. The illusion is that you see things differently from their essence because what you see is constantly changing. One might see something as a table, the other as wood.

Everything is made from one essence, but different names are given to the many forms that it takes. The world that you see is just name and form. If you can see beyond the name and form, you see the truth.

From this vantage what is seen superficially is unreal. Each may have its own reality from a worldly vision, but the true inner vision will tell you that it's all the same. Even the you who sees mundane things is not different from that Absolute One. When Sri Ramakrishna was trying to explain the meaning of the same Upanishad, he said, "Yes, that may all be true, but I don't want it."

Why? Imagine an ant who has discovered a hill of sugar. With great joy he concentrates on the sugar hill, eating there constantly. You become what you concentrate on. "I don't want to become sugar," says the happy devotee. "I just want to be the ant in the sugar hill, and keep on eating. I don't want Shankara's philosophy. I'm even a little frightened of that. If I am going to become sugar myself, why should I even come here to eat it? No I don't want to lose my individuality totally."

This is another approach. A devotee wants to be a devotee always. He wants to go near or become parallel to God, to be similar, or even be in His likeness. But he doesn't want to become God, because there's no charm in life then, no love-making between God and the devotee anymore. "I can't enjoy loving my God," he says, "if I am going to become God myself." That's why Ramakrishna taught that the *advaita* philosophy, which says we should realize we are all one with the Absolute, is a little dry. If that happens, who is there to enjoy it? There's no individual anymore. There ends the matter.

But the path of devotion is so beautiful. There is charm in life. You can still be separate and enjoy it. With that devotion you can come so close to God you may be frightened. That's good. You shouldn't be afraid of God as some extraneous being, but when the finite faces the unthinkable magnitude of the infinite and is petrified, true humility is born, and the devotee knows the whole world is the Lord's temple.

Bhakti or devotional Yoga might seem even better than *Jnana* Yoga, the path of wisdom through self-analysis. But devotion without wisdom is not devotion at all. While you're having love with God, you should have wisdom, too. Standing apart and loving Him is really beautiful. A devotee always wants that. But the fact remains; the devotee and the Devoted are one and the same. Know who you ultimately are even while you stay separate to enjoy more happiness in life.

Unless you are separate you can't even know about God's mercy and love. One Tamil saint sang, "Oh Lord, you know I am

Your child. My nature is to commit sins. May I remind You of Your nature—which is to pardon all my mistakes. My nature is to keep on making mistakes, and Your nature is to keep on forgiving me." What a fine excuse he has!

Shankara taught that we are all one with God, but didn't want to feel that way all the time. In his personal practice he was a devotee, a great worshipper of God seen as the Mother. He established many shrines for Her and wrote more poems as a devotee than as an *advaitin*. At one point he looked at Her, and said, "Mother, the world has seen many bad children, but never a mother who does not forgive them. You are my Mother, I am Your child. Even when I am bad, how can You not forgive me? Accept me because there can be bad children but never a bad mother."

That is a devotee's sure approach: a request, even a demand. With such devotion there is the confidence that whatever I do, ultimately God will transform me, and save me from my bad habits. Once we have such confidence in God we'll see the protective hands. Then we'll feel whatever happens is His business. If we have faith in God, we need have no fear in anything and we will see God in everything, too.

Approach God first as if you are doing something and you want help. Ultimately, you will end up feeling that He is working through you. Then just be an instrument in His hands. Another great sage used to remind Him, "Lord, don't you remember that day when I gave myself completely in Your hands? Not only my body and my property, but myself totally. I gave everything of mine into Your hands. Do You remember that? Well, in that case, can there be any difficulty for me today? Not at all. Should I worry about anything? No. You have taken me as Your instrument. You are living in me as body and mind, even as this life. You are handling me. If people should say of me, 'Hey, you are doing something bad,' why should I worry? You do everything through me. Or if somebody says to me, 'Oh, you are a truly great person,' I know who really is doing it. Others may not know, but I know. Therefore, You are responsible for everything —good or bad—that happens through me, because I have resigned everything to You."

That is becoming an instrument in the hands of God. In day-to-day law, you see the same thing. If someone is murdered, will the FBI put the gun in prison? They look for the person who held the gun. Of course, being an instrument is no excuse to do unkind things. But if you have given everything to God, you need not be bothered by censure. Nor can you come forward to take the reward for good actions, either. Both belong to God. That is the approach of a devotee. He is free in the hands of God. God will make use of him any way He wants. And people will see God through the actions of his devotees, as we see electricity through lamps or radios.

Such devotion requires absolute faith, but it need not be blind faith. The mind should also be convinced. The reason for faith can be proven logically. When you say, "I do something," what is actually happening? Can you say, "I am lifting the book and putting it on the table with my own hands?" To lift the book you need some strength. Where do you get the strength? If you are asked to fast for fifteen days, you may not have the strength to get up or talk or even look at someone. You get your strength by eating and breathing. Your strength comes from outside, from nature, from the food and the air you take in.

Who gives that? If you reply, "nature," who is the cause for nature? That unseen force. God produced the food. You ate it, but who digested it for you? God again. With His energy you prepared the food. With that energy you cook it, chew it, and digest it. With His energy you can lift a pen and write or put it down. Who is speaking to you now? The credit should go to Him, not to me. We don't always realize that and try to take credit ourselves.

Something is taking good care of your breath and your life, because that unseen force wants you to live longer. Why? Probably to fulfill His work. He has a cosmic plan. He has to do it through you as His instrument. So He takes good care of the instrument. When your part of the work is over, He will not send you any more air. That will be your final breath.

All of this demonstrates that we are not even living for ourselves by ourselves. There is one common Cosmic Consciousness which makes us live. In this respect I speak of "we" as bodies and minds because that is how we function on the physical and mental levels. With such identification we can say God is working in us and through us. But if we identify ourselves as that image of God, then we say God is using that body and mind. Either way we can be happy.

The great devotee Hanuman once addressed God, "Often I live thinking that I am the body or the mind. Whenever I think that, let me be Your servant. If I think I am the soul, let me think I'm part of You. But when I think that I am the pure Self, let me think that I am You."

You function on different levels. If you are using the physical body, think of yourself as a Karma Yogi dedicating all your actions to Him. If you use your heart, think of yourself as a Bhakti Yogi who is an instrument of God. If you are using your head, think of yourself as a Jnana Yogi who does not identify with anything less than the true Self. If you blend all together, think of yourself as a Raja Yogi integrating all the approaches.

42. What We Call Holy

There is only one God who is our Lord, who is the life in us. We are that image. God is always one because there is only one God who is called by different names. We talk in different languages about one truth.

You are the essence. When it is divided it becomes nonsense. Like rain in the river going back to the ocean, every drop of water that wants to go back to its source is a religious seeker. God above is like completely distilled water, the Absolute One. When it falls down to this side of the river, He becomes Israel's God and is called Heavenly Father. On the other side they call Him Allah. If He falls in the Himalayas, they call Him Siva.

The same is true of what we call holy. "God" is just a common term generally approved by almost all religions. By that we mean a Cosmic Power or Intelligence. Though we use different words and names, we mean the same thing. The names of God are also holy because the name and the one who belongs to the name are inseparable.

God is pleased with any name you give Him, just like a baby who comes to a big family. That child will be called in ten different ways. Mama calls him one way, Papa another, younger sister still a third affectionate name. God doesn't care what we call Him, but rather what feeling we are using. He is interested in our hearts, not our heads. Because of our limitations we give Him different names and see different forms. Out of His greatness, He lets us do that.

Certainly you can call God "She." "Thou art That," say the sages. Probably because men began interpreting this, they thought of God as "He." Some think of God as "She." Why only think of God as "Father?" He can be "Brother," "Sister," "Friend," or "Beloved." Actually, God is all these and more. Choose a particular relationship for your personal worship of God. If you love your father more, you might naturally call God your beloved Father. If you are frightened of your father and love your mother, then you may think God is a beautiful Mother. Approach Him any way you like, He won't say no to you.

Human beings may imagine God as a superhuman form with six heads and twelve arms. In Hinduism you see that. It's natural for the mind to think like that.

If a buffalo wanted to approach God, certainly he would not expect to see God as a man because buffaloes are not treated well by men. The buffalo would probably think of God as a great buffalo with four horns and two tails.

According to Vedic teachings, all individuals—women and men—are the brides and God is the only bridegroom. We are all wooing Him. We are the feminine, only He is the masculine. God is like a static force that expresses itself through activity. All creation is a manifestation of that static force. This is nature or the Mother. Only the Mother can conceive and deliver the baby, not the Father. He is not for activity. The entire universe is Mother. In Hindu mythology, goddesses are always glorified before their consorts because without the power the static force is useless.

There are people in India who worship Siva as the Almighty. But if you go to Bengal, you will see they worship the goddess, Shakti, as the predominant or Almighty One. Maybe you have seen pictures of Shakti dancing on the chest of Siva, who is just lying like a corpse. Did you understand what they mean? Siva is a corpse without Shakti; a powerless God is no God at all.

Don't misunderstand, Shakti cannot dance without Siva. They are not two different gods, but different aspects of the one God. Siva is expressing or making Himself known as Shakti. Without that glittering, shining, brilliant surface, a diamond is just a stone. Without the light, the stone is not a precious gem. But without the stone, there is no brilliant light. They are inseparable. One part is visible because of the other. Siva cannot express Himself without Shakti, who cannot dance without Siva.

It's something like a dynamo. Unmoving, it is useless and harmless, because it is producing no current. It's just there. But the minute it starts moving, you immediately put a fence around it: "Danger, 30,000 volts. Stay clear." What good is a motionless dynamo? We need the current, the Shakti.

If you ever see a drawing of Lord Vishnu, known also as Narayana, you will always see his beloved Lakshmi residing in his heart. These are just symbols showing that without manifestation the Lord cannot be used, understood, or realized. The manifestation or the power is the goddess part. God is omnipresent, but if He doesn't manifest Himself into all these things of the world, there's no charming play of life and no way to realize God.

It's easy to talk about enlightenment, but just to hear or read about the truth is not enough. You don't pay to read the menu. What good is anything until you have actually tasted it? Oneness is to be experienced in the complete silence of mind, the realization of God can't be grasped totally by the mind. If you experience oneness, when you try to describe it you must use the limited mind to approximate what is happening beyond mind.

That's why Buddhists don't even talk about God. Lord Buddha himself was the son of Hindu parents. Buddha must have been aware of all the calamities and chaos from religions. There were hundreds of sects then chopping off each others' heads in the name of God. So he said, "No, I won't add more to that. Let me stop this nonsense. Why talk about it? Let people experience that."

Toward the end of his life, Buddha noticed Ananda, one of his senior devotees, standing nearby looking a little sad. So he asked: "Ananda are you sad because I am leaving this body?"

"No, sir. But there is still one unanswered question that saddens me."

"Ask."

"Sir, you never said anything about God. Does it mean you deny God?"

"Ananda, did I ever deny God?"

"No, sir, you didn't. In that case, can I say that you accept God?"

"Ananda, did I ever accept God?"

He neither denied nor accepted. What does it mean? He didn't want to talk about that which cannot be well described. The day man started talking about God, he created all kinds of religious quarrels. God may have made man in His image, but men with their different egos have differed in creating God's image. That's why each one has his own God and fights about it with others. It's better not to talk and just realize God yourself.

As you realize, you rise above all your earlier imaginings of what God is, and you become one with That. Until that happens, just believe there is something beyond which you are trying to reach. You will grow. In order to know what it is, follow the way.

Since Buddha would not talk of the experience his devotees asked him, "Then what do you want us to do?"

"Go ahead, practice. Do these things. You know that there is sorrow in the world and misery. If you want to get out of it, discover the cause for the misery. To get out of this suffering, eradicate all your personal wants. Free yourself. Liberate yourself from all these wrong identifications. Become almost naked so that nothing binds you. *Nirvana* is nakedness. The soul must be naked. The mind must be clear of all identifications and associations—undisturbed."

"And once we do that, what will happen?"

"I need not tell you."

If you want, you may choose to put yourself in God's hands through your own intelligence. It is for that purpose that free will has been given you. Your first and foremost duty as a human being is to recognize that spiritual force functioning within.

If you renounce all personal desires, the mind will no longer be tossed about and you will be able to realize the Self within. Giving to others without expecting anything in return is the key. That is the essence of every religion. It is the essence of Yoga. When you do that, things come by themselves to you. Maybe not at first when you are being tested. You may become even a pauper for some time. If the mind is pure you will say, "It doesn't matter, whatever I have, I give. Nobody is forcing me. I'm not looking for rewards."

When the Cosmic Consciousness is satisfied that you are really a great channel, it will send you more and more. You will realize the nature of God. The Omnipresent, All-merciful will work through you, and you will realize that God is within. Having that realization, you will see God everywhere in everything. You will see that the entire creation is a manifestation of God. You will learn to love all humanity, nature, animals, and plants. Then your service to God will be service to humanity, service to all the world. You won't have to *do* anything. Just by being your Self you will be loving and serving God.

The easiest way to begin is just to associate with people who do this. In time this will lead to different practices. Your meditations will reveal God within, you will go out and serve. One who practices meditation and the other disciplines is like a barber who is constantly sharpening his blade as he prepares to do the shaving which is service in the world. If you only serve, your blade will become dull. Everytime your service gets dull, go within and sharpen the blade of your awareness. Then go back out and serve some more. Maybe one day they will invent something that will keep the blade sharp in the midst of shaving. That's the way of the realized ones who see God constantly while living in the world and serving everyone.

43. *Truth Is One, Paths Are Many*

There is one Cosmic Essence, all pervading, all knowing, all powerful. As such it has no limited form and name, but can take any. This One is the cause for all these many things that we call His creation or manifestation. Therefore, all beings are essentially pure, calm, and divine.

By communicating with this One, or by realizing this, we can have better understanding, better living, and greater capabilities. We may call this One God, Brahman, Adonoi, Allah, Father, Mother, The Thing-in-Itself, Cosmic Consciousness, Divine Essence, and so on and on endlessly. This One can be approached by any form or symbol to suit the taste of the individual.

But we cannot communicate with or realize this One without a clean, calm mind as our instrument. And without a sound body, it is almost impossible to maintain a calm mind, at least in the beginning. By nature, the mind and body are happy and healthy, peaceful and at ease. It is our duty to maintain this ease and peace. We can do this by being certain all our actions—both physical and mental—are perfect, causing no disturbance to the mind.

All the different religions, either directly or indirectly, are helping us achieve this peace and ease. Unless individuals find this ease first, it cannot be realized throughout the world. We should resolve to lead a peaceful and ease-filled life, dedicating that to the welfare of the world.

Imagine a summit that can be approached by many different routes. One man starts from the eastern side; the other from the west. As they are climbing they won't see each other. But if they both have walkie-talkies, one might call to the other: "Hey, where are you going?"

"I'm going up to the summit."

"Hmmm? I am also going to the summit, but this is certainly the road."

"No, you fool. Come to this side. Follow my path."

"No, this is the only way to the summit."

In a way, both are right. But at least until one of them reaches his goal, he may not understand that the other is also on his way to the summit. When he gets to the top he will see the other also climbing. "Oh, I see now. Both paths come to the same place. I was shouting and finding fault with him, demanding that he come onto my path. Thank God, he didn't believe me and go all the way down to the bottom again, walk around and start climbing anew. It would have taken much longer for him."

If you know both roads are ultimately going to the same place, you can easily admit, "You are also right. We'll meet there. You take your route; I'll take mine." But in order to know that, either you believe others who have told you, or you must go to that summit yourself. Until then, don't distract the other person.

That's universality. As long as you are a seeker after God, go toward Him. That's your only business. You are a traveler. Perhaps you have a teacher who has told you the way. You have no business trying to teach others until you reach your goal. You can teach *after* you reach God. Then you will surely not disturb the other person's faith. Otherwise, it is like the blind leading the blind.

No two rivers are exactly alike in quality. They have different names, shades, and tastes. But they are all running to the same source. When they reach the ocean can you distinguish the Ganges from the Missouri, the Euphrates from the Hudson? They lose their individuality because they become one.

Whatever path you choose according to your temperament and taste, stay with that consistently. Though God can be approached through any form or name, if you keep changing from one idea of God to another, you won't progress at all. In time the idea you choose is accepted by your mind. Eventually, the mind itself will assume the form or qualities of the one you are worshipping or meditating on. The worshipper ultimately gets the qualities of the Worshipped. But if you keep on changing, the mind will not get those good qualities. You can't travel on ten roads at the same time, even if they're all going to Rome.

It's the same with a personal mantra. If a teacher gives you a mantra, you should think it is the only one for you; don't even think of other mantras. Just repeat it and chant it. When you meditate it is yours. It's like a girl who catches a boy and makes him her husband. She won't treat anyone else as she treats him. Treat your choice of God as your most beloved.

Even in devotion we can be prostitutes. If we have one form of worship today, another tomorrow, and still another on the third day, we will not get anywhere. It's like digging a well in a hundred places. Nowhere will we get water. Thousands may be walking on the way, each with his own method. All of them may be right, but we each have to stick to one path.

At the same time a truly religious person will never condemn anybody else's way. If you want to know God, raise yourself to that level. It takes a thief to know a thief. It takes a saint to know a saint. If you put someone else down, you just limit yourself. Sometimes people are fanatical about their faith. The converted or newfound religionists are often worse than others. They are overenthusiastic at the beginning and are not yet strong enough in their own faith to understand that others are also going to the summit by different paths. We are all the sons and daughters of God. Every one is chosen. But even in spiritual practice one man's food is another man's poison.

Be devoted to the religion from which you came. It's something like your mother. I have only one Mother. I can't have more than one. She is very beloved to me. But because I love her should I say, "only my mother is a chaste lady?" You would hate me. As I love my mother, you love yours.

Any religion that quarrels with another religion is not truly a religion. Religion means all-embracing, no quarrels. If ever a person calls himself religious and denies the other's way or religion, know for sure he doesn't yet understand his own religion.

Just teaching one type of approach won't work in this age. Now we must show people the universal approach. Many people are dissatisfied in their own religions because the disciplines, rituals, and rules are presented without explanation. That won't work today. I am really glad to see the present generation questioning everything. "Why should we do it? What's the purpose behind it?" In fact, most of the spiritual practices and religious rituals have lost their meaning. People do them mechanically.

Rituals are simply practical hints or external replicas of what should happen within you. If you take flowers to church, it's a way of bringing your affection to God. If you bring fruits, you are bringing the fruits of your actions. In India they may bring two bananas—offering the results of both the good actions and the bad actions. "I don't want anything God. I offer it all to You." Sometimes there is a screen or curtain before the altar. When that is opened you are in the presence of God, you have transcended your personal ego which was a veil before you.

Rituals themselves will not bring peace or communion. The whole idea of all such ceremonies is to remove disturbances that hide the truth so you can realize. If religious rituals are properly understood, they may help you. But they can also bind you, if you do them without knowing the meaning. That's why so many people are discarding them. Why do you light a candle at an altar or to begin the Sabbath? Is God blind? Can't He see without the light? That light is the symbol of the spiritual light you have ignited within yourself as you come into His presence. The light of truth should never be allowed to go out—that's the eternal light.

If you come close to that eternal light, you, too, will catch its fire; ego burns away and you are enlightened. Your individuality disappears, you become one with the whole. You are never separated from God. This is the secret significance of all these symbols and rituals. But the mind cannot understand anything without symbols. So rituals and scriptures are like ladders to climb up on. One great sage once said, "There are two kinds of people who do not need scriptures or dogma. One is the fool and one is full." The fool doesn't know how or care to read. He might use the scriptures as a pillow. The full one already knows and doesn't need a book.

When you are full you can throw away the book. When you climb upstairs why cling onto the ladder that got you there—the rituals and religious paraphernalia? They can be very helpful to lift you, but then they might become bondage. Some people sit there worshipping the ladder itself: "Oh my beautiful ladder, please take me up." Even some holy scriptures have been treated this way, covered with gold and velvet cases, placed on the altar, and worshipped. I have seen many people worshipping the *Bhagavad Gita* that way. They know nothing about what's inside. Holy books and rituals are to help you realize the spirit within, to feel the oneness and the universality.

Follow your religion but try to learn the real purpose of all its rituals and traditions. Let the rituals help you reach your goal, which is the fundamental purpose of all religions. Offer up your individuality and recognize your spiritual oneness with everyone and the whole universe.

44. Cosmic Consciousness

All paths lead home. Who lives in the middle of that home? OM. And who lives on either side? HE. So whenever you think of OM you're at home. That's why in Sri Patanjali's Yoga sutras he says the name of the Cosmic One is Om.

Really, it's not even Om. That's just the name we give to something which is expressed. More literally it's like a steady "Hmmm," that humming sound of life throughout the universe. Probably you would pronounce it "aum." It begins with "ah." When you just open your mouth you naturally pronounce "ah," the beginning of all audible sounds. You don't have to do anything with the mouth, the tongue, or move the lips—"ah" just comes.

That's why every language begins with the sound "ah." And once that first audible sound is made, we call that the creation. Then it has to survive, which it does with the next part: "ooh" just rolls to the lips and continues until the end. And, naturally, anything that is produced must have an end; "mmm," which is the destruction or the involution. Thus, Creation—ah; preservation—oo; destruction—mm. Put it all together and it becomes Om. So all creation, preservation, and destruction are seen in Om. All the sounds and words ever produced are in the middle of that Om sound. If you utter any sound and analyze it, you can condense it into these three parts.

Om is the beginning. Om is also the end. The entire creation began and continues in Om, and probably one day it will end in

Om. That is the word which was in the beginning and which is with God and will be with God. In the Bible it's called the Word. In Hindu scriptures it's called the sound of the Absolute God. All religions seem to know it. Some pronounce it as Amen, or Omayn or Ameen, or just Om or hum. When a static dynamo starts rotating, the first thing you hear is the hum. So when God as the static or unmanifested One wanted to set Himself in motion, he just hummed first. That's why in the beginning there was the Word, or this sound. He became aware of Himself and wanted to see things expressed. The very first manifestation of the absolute omnipresent, omniscient, and omnipotent One is sound, the most subtle of manifestations.

That means even before sound there is an Absolute state in which there is neither sound nor light nor motion. It's impossible to define because it's infinite. The mind's capacity is finite. Volumes have been written about God in many languages, countries, and faiths, but all are talking about the same Cosmic One which is undefinable. All that we can say is that God first expressed Himself as sound vibrations.

He created the whole universe with that sound. Or you could say He created the whole universe as sound, which is where religion and science agree. Scientists have also discovered that everything you see—and even what you cannot see—is nothing but atomic vibrations. Beyond the protons, neutrons, and electrons there seems to be a consciousness that doesn't want to come into our test tubes. Although scientists can't yet pinpoint it, they are suggesting that maybe it is pure energy or sound.

Form follows sound. Sound itself is a very subtle form, which gives rise to more concrete forms that can be seen. When sound vibrations become a little more concrete, sound becomes a point, and from many points come forms. Today photographs of sounds can be made which show different geometrical figures. Scientists can also send sound against a fine area of sand spread over glass and see the pattern formed there. This shows that sound has form.

That atomic vibration is in everything, whether it appears to be moving or unmoving. Science says all is made from the atom. God says all comes from Adam. In Sanskrit, they call it "Atman" which is the true Self. See how close we always are? Everything has consciousness because the vital energy of that hum or first manifestation is causing movement or current everywhere. That movement is omnipresent in every atom. Because of that force in the atom the neutron attracts the electrons and they go round and round. This is the cosmic attraction toward the opposite pole or opposite sex which is part of nature. This is what makes electricity or current. Like electric power, God steps Himself down to us from the Absolute through sound and then form until we can benefit from Him.

We are all like gadgets plugging into His power, which he has limited so that we can make use of Him. There is just this constant flow of the Cosmic energy, or Universal Consciousness, that we call God. It flows multivariously and in so doing forms different waves or bubbles. Some of those forms or bubbles are we.

Just as waves form when wind blows over the ocean, or ice forms when the temperature changes, we, too, are formed as little bubbles. We are all here now, but we don't know when we'll break out of these little individual forms. A bubble in an ocean wave may last a few seconds while we have a life span of seventy to a hundred years. He is a bubble called Mr. So-and-so. I am the bubble they now call Swami. The bubble maintains its shape because the air inside and the air outside is of equal pressure. When one increases or decreases, the bubble breaks. The same thing will happen to us. It's the law of nature.

We are all different shapes of the same matter. Through Yoga you can experience this yourself; don't just read about it and nod. When you personally realize it, you yourself will have become this basic truth. You can do so while you're a separate or individual bubble, but later you won't think of yourself as an individual. You will have become absorbed in the Whole. If you want to know God a hundred per cent in His true way, become That. If a drop wants to know the depth of the ocean, it should become the ocean. Slowly the joy at certain levels of your meditation will dissolve into something universal. Then when you come back to your individual self, what can you say? There are no words to express it.

In the absolute sense, the real is that which is always permanent. The unreal is that which changes. Using water to represent that essence, you can say the waves, spray, bubbles, and ice are all unreal; only the water itself is real. That doesn't mean you should fight with somebody who insists it is only a wave. Of course it is while it has that form, but you should have the larger —or double—vision. Maybe the other person only has single vision. When people get caught up in the names and forms they get into trouble.

Name and form are superficial differences. Over and above name and form is absolute existence, consciousness, and bliss. Everything has these five aspects: existence, knowledge, joy, name, and form. Look at this page of paper, for example. Its essence is pulp. It is now expressing itself as paper, which was cut into form to be printed on so you can enjoy it. The whole world is just name and form. Name and form are just for fun, like playing hide and seek for enjoyment. But if you forget that and get caught up in the names and forms, you will suffer from that ignorance.

A chess board is made out of wood, as are all the pieces which are cut into different shapes to play the game. Call them pawns, kings, queens, castles, knights, or bishops and give them different names and forms to play the game—they are all cut from the same stock. We, too, are all chips off the same block.

Once God told a story: what a terrible dream I had. I thought I was something different. I dreamed I was so hungry, I was forced to eat a dead dog, and out of hunger I called to God, "Lord, how can you make me do this?" All of a sudden I woke up and realized I was—I am—God.

Sometimes a dream is so intense the physical body gets into it. You take the corner of the pillow and start biting it. Someone calls, "Hey there. You have sumptuous food and you're eating the pillow." The only way to stop from eating the pillow is to wake up. Someone must alert you, shake you. A similar thing is happening in our lives. Some are in deep sleep and don't know what they're doing. Most are just dreaming that there is darkness and their eyes are closed. Some people are daydreamers. People dream and forget their true nature. In the dream they think "This is my house, my land, my factory, my child"—all the *mines*. That's the dream, forgetting our true nature and identifying instead with so many other things.

Pleasant dreams and dreadful dreams are like tricks, mental hallucinations. How can we wake the dreamers? Nice soft words? They will just sleep more. Give them a nice kick. But who can wake the sleeper? The one who is already awake. The enlightened ones kick us. Once we awaken, we say, "I was never hungry. I was not unhappy. I was not this body. It isn't mine." We are not the body or the mind. We are not even the soul which is a reflection of the Self.

You are the Self. The Self never undergoes any change. It's always pure and calm. It just *is*—right here and now. It doesn't need religion. What does it have to go back to? Does the Self need to realize its Self? When did God forget Himself? That One is omnipresent. The Self doesn't want to find its Self because it never lost it.

At the point of realization there is no ego. That's when the shadow realizes it's a shadow. The soul, which is the reflection of the Self, wants to practice all these religions to find the origin of mind in order to discover the answer to the question, "Who am I?" But when it finds the answer, the "I" is not there. That's *maya* —the one that is never existing. Who is *maya?* You see the footprints of the duck on the sky—it's all sound. My mother is barren. My mother has no child at all. This is a description of *maya*—something that is not there but appears to be so. That is what we call ego.

But down on our level, all these appearances seem true. What use is this theoretical knowledge? We should at least know it. Put it in our pockets and save it. One day it will help a lot.

Why did God create this material world and put us into this game? The only one who can fully answer this question is the one who made everything. But when you see Him you probably will say, "I've been meaning to ask You this and that, but now that I see You, I don't have anything to ask." Just find out as soon as possible where He is and question Him if you can.

Epilogue: Old Wine—New Bottle

I've given you some points. Apply whatever is suitable to your life. Please know that I am not just quoting books or simply producing some prerecorded ideas. What is here comes from my heart, from my very life. I tell you what I feel. I want you to enjoy what I enjoy. If something is not possible for me, I won't ask you to do it. But of this I'm positive: You can always be healthy and happy and blissful. There's no doubt about it. Nothing can disturb your peace if you keep a few of these teachings in your life and don't try to find any short cuts. Don't expect miracles. The only short cut is to remold your life.

Stay away from anything that will disturb you. All Yoga practices deal with the mind. It is the mind that is creating all your troubles. You can train it and use it to your own higher advantage—that is why it was given to you. And you can achieve this by the practice of Yoga anywhere and everywhere. Ultimately, you must find that peace everywhere. You don't have to talk about it; just do it, live it. The real Sat-Chid-Ananda exists within every human being. The goal is to realize that Self; realize that peace, joy, and love; realize that light—all different names for the same experience. I have given you everything you need for a happy, healthy, harmonious, successful life which leads to final liberation. It's up to you to take the tools I have given and put them to good use.

All I teach is that you learn to be selfless. Your life can be a beautiful fruit for all humanity to enjoy. You can retain the God who is already in you in the form of peace and joy. And when you shine with peace, you expose to that light not only yourself, but other people as well. Let people see something beautiful in you, something genuine in you. Let God be born in you. That's my prayer. Let it begin with you, then let it spread to your community, to your country, and ultimately to the entire globe.

If by any chance, I have hurt your feelings by my words, I very much request that you pardon me. I am still human. Maybe I am overanxious to reach you. Yoga is really the same old wine, but in different bottles. Nobody can say anything new about the eternal and unchanging truth. But minds change in each age, so we must present the ancient wisdom to satisfy this age.

I really feel we are coming into a great spiritual age. I see an awakening. I have tremendous faith in you people who are the new hope. The world is going to be a heaven, no doubt. There may still be a few undesirable people—it would be boring otherwise—but the majority will be Yogis. I have complete confidence in it.

May God who is the truth, the peace, and the joy, who is all virtue within us and everywhere, bless us with the understanding to come together and live together and make this world a beautiful heaven. May you all experience perfect health, peace, prosperity, and bliss.